TEACHER'S PET PUBLICATIONS

PUZZLE PACK
for
Tuck Everlasting

based on the book by
Natalie Babbitt

Written by
William T. Collins

© 2005 Teacher's Pet Publications
All Rights Reserved

The materials in this packet are copyrighted
by Teacher's Pet Publications, Inc.

These pages may be duplicated by the purchaser
for use in the purchaser's own classroom.

Copying any of these materials and distributing them
for any other purpose is a violation of the copyright laws.

© 2005 Teacher's Pet Publications, Inc.
www.tpet.com

INTRODUCTION
If you already own the LitPlan for this title, this Puzzle Pack will refresh your Unit Resource Materials and Vocabulary Resource Materials sections plus give you additional materials you can substitute into the tests.If you do not already have a complete LitPlan, these pages will give you some supplemental materials to use with your own plan. There are two main groups of materials: one set for unit words (such as characters' names, symbols, places, etc.) and one set for vocabulary words associated with the book.

WORD LIST
There is a word list for both the unit words and the vocabulary words. These lists show you which words are being used in the materials and the clues or definitions being used for those words. You may want to give students a word list with clues/definitions to help them, or you may want students to only have a word list (without clues/definitions) if you want them to work a little harder. Both are available for duplication. The word lists can also be your "calling key" for the bingo games.

FILL IN THE BLANK AND MATCHING
There are 4 each of the fill in the blank and matching worksheets for both the unit and vocabulary words. These pages can be used either as extra worksheets for students or as objective parts of a unit test. They can be done individually if students need extra help or as a whole class activity to review the material covered.

MAGIC SQUARES
The magic squares not only reinforce the material covered but also work on reasoning and math skills. Many teachers have told us that their students really enjoy doing these!

WORD SEARCH PUZZLES
The word search words go in all directions, as indicated on your answer keys. Two of the word search puzzles have the clues listed rather than the words. This makes the puzzle a little more difficult, but it reinforces the material better. Two word search puzzles have words only for students who find the clue puzzles too difficult.

CROSSWORD PUZZLES
Both unit and vocabulary word sections have 4 crossword puzzles.

BINGO CARDS
There are 32 individual bingo cards for the unit words and 32 individual bingo cards for the vocabulary words. You can use your word list as a "call list," calling the words at random and marking them off of your list as you go, or you could use the flash cards by cutting them apart and drawing the words at random from a hat (or box or whatever). To make a better review, you might ask for the definition and spelling of each word as you call it out–or you could call out the definitions and have students tell you the words they need to look for on the puzzle.

JUGGLE LETTERS
The vocabulary juggle letter game is intended to help students learn the spellings of the words. One sheet has the definitions listed on it as an extra help for students who need it or to reinforce the definitions if you choose to do so.

FLASH CARDS
We've included a set of vocabulary flash cards you can duplicate, cut, and fold for your students. Some teachers make a few sets for general use by the class; others make a set for each student. Some teachers duplicate them for each student and have the students cut & fold their own. You can cut out just the words and put them in a hat, have each student pick out one word and write the definition and a sentence for that word. Students then swap words and papers, with the next student adding a sentence of his own under the last one. You can have students swap as many times as you like. Each time the student will read the sentences written prior to his own and then add a sentence. You can cut out the words and definitions separately and play "I Have; Who Has?" Each student in the room draws a word and definition. The first student says, "I have (the name of the word). Who has the definition?" The student with the definition reads it then says, "I have (the name of the vocabulary word she has). Who has the definition?" The round continues until all words and definitions have been given.

Tuck Everlasting Word List

No.	Word	Clue/Definition
1.	ANGUS	He hated being stuck in time
2.	ANNA	Miles's daughter
3.	ASH	Giant tree in the center of the wood
4.	AUGUST	Month beginning the live-long year
5.	BABBITT	Author
6.	BARN	Color of Tucks' home: ___-red
7.	BLACK	The man in the yellow suit wore a ___ hat
8.	BLANKET	Winnie wrapped up in one to fool the constable
9.	BLEW	The gallows ___ over in the storm
10.	BUGGY	Tucks' transportation to Treegap after seventy years
11.	CARPENTRY	Miles's vocation
12.	CAT	It died a natural death
13.	CEMETERY	Where Tucks discovered Winnie's fate
14.	CONSTABLE	He arrested Mae
15.	CURSE	Endless life was a ___ to Angus
16.	DEVIL	Miles's wife thought he sold his soul to him
17.	EIGHTY	Number of years Tucks remained unchanged: ____-seven
18.	ELVES	Grandma thought they made the music
19.	FIREFLIES	Winnie liked to catch these
20.	FOSTERS	They owned the wood
21.	HORSE	Stolen by stranger
22.	IRON	Surrounds touch-me-not cottage: ___ fence
23.	JAIL	Winnie took Mae's place there
24.	JESSE	Gave a bottle of spring water to Winnie
25.	KIDNAPPED	Tucks did this to Winnie
26.	LIGHTNING	Flashed when the window came out
27.	MAE	She crawled through the jailhouse window
28.	MIDNIGHT	Meeting time for Jesse and Winnie
29.	MILES	He wished to do something important
30.	MUSIC	Mae's prettiest possession: ___ box
31.	NAILS	Miles removed them from the window
32.	ONE	Mae's philosophy: ___ day at a time
33.	PEBBLES	Were stacked up to hide the spring
34.	POND	It explained the cycle of life
35.	RAIN	Began when Mae got out of window
36.	RIFLE	Mae hit the stranger with this
37.	ROWBOAT	Winnie went fishing in this
38.	SELL	Stranger wanted to do this with the spring water
39.	SEVENTEEN	Jesse's age
40.	SEVENTY	Number of years since the jailhouse escape
41.	SPRING	It spurted the fountain of youth
42.	STRANGER	Wore a yellow suit
43.	STUCK	How Angus described their situation
44.	SUIT	Worn by the stranger: yellow ___
45.	SWIM	What boys did when they got home
46.	T	Letter carved in the ash tree by Angus
47.	TEN	Time between visits by Tucks' sons: ___ years
48.	TOAD	Everlasting amphibian
49.	TOUCH	The Foster's cottage: ___-Me-Not
50.	TOYS	Angus and Mae made them to sell: wooden ___
51.	TREEGAP	Town near the wood

Copyrighted

Tuck Everlasting Word List Continued

No.	Word	Clue/Definition
52.	TROUT	Miles threw it back because of Winnie: rainbow ___
53.	TWENTY	Miles's age: ___-two
54.	WATER	Winnie poured bottled ___ over toad.
55.	WHEEL	Center of universe
56.	WINDOW	Miles removed it from the jail
57.	WINNIE	Became a hero among her peers: ___ Foster
58.	WOOD	Given in exchange for Winnie's rescue
59.	YEAR	Began when the Tucks drank from the spring: live-long ___

Tuck Everlasting Fill In The Blanks 1

_____ 1. Given in exchange for Winnie's rescue

_____ 2. Began when Mae got out of window

_____ 3. Mae's prettiest possession: ___ box

_____ 4. Letter carved in the ash tree by Angus

_____ 5. Grandma thought they made the music

_____ 6. How Angus described their situation

_____ 7. Angus and Mae made them to sell: wooden ___

_____ 8. Miles's vocation

_____ 9. Miles removed them from the window

_____ 10. The gallows ___ over in the storm

_____ 11. Center of universe

_____ 12. It explained the cycle of life

_____ 13. Number of years Tucks remained unchanged: ____-seven

_____ 14. Month beginning the live-long year

_____ 15. Mae hit the stranger with this

_____ 16. Were stacked up to hide the spring

_____ 17. Winnie liked to catch these

_____ 18. Became a hero among her peers: ____ Foster

_____ 19. The man in the yellow suit wore a ___ hat

_____ 20. Author

Tuck Everlasting Fill In The Blanks 1 Answer Key

WOOD	1. Given in exchange for Winnie's rescue
RAIN	2. Began when Mae got out of window
MUSIC	3. Mae's prettiest possession: ___ box
T	4. Letter carved in the ash tree by Angus
ELVES	5. Grandma thought they made the music
STUCK	6. How Angus described their situation
TOYS	7. Angus and Mae made them to sell: wooden ___
CARPENTRY	8. Miles's vocation
NAILS	9. Miles removed them from the window
BLEW	10. The gallows ___ over in the storm
WHEEL	11. Center of universe
POND	12. It explained the cycle of life
EIGHTY	13. Number of years Tucks remained unchanged: ____-seven
AUGUST	14. Month beginning the live-long year
RIFLE	15. Mae hit the stranger with this
PEBBLES	16. Were stacked up to hide the spring
FIREFLIES	17. Winnie liked to catch these
WINNIE	18. Became a hero among her peers: ____ Foster
BLACK	19. The man in the yellow suit wore a ___ hat
BABBITT	20. Author

Tuck Everlasting Fill In The Blanks 2

_____ 1. Number of years since the jailhouse escape

_____ 2. How Angus described their situation

_____ 3. The gallows ___ over in the storm

_____ 4. Angus and Mae made them to sell: wooden ___

_____ 5. Winnie went fishing in this

_____ 6. Miles's age: ___-two

_____ 7. Author

_____ 8. She crawled through the jailhouse window

_____ 9. Winnie wrapped up in one to fool the constable

_____ 10. Giant tree in the center of the wood

_____ 11. It spurted the fountain of youth

_____ 12. What boys did when they got home

_____ 13. Stranger wanted to do this with the spring water

_____ 14. Began when the Tucks drank from the spring: live-long ____

_____ 15. Number of years Tucks remained unchanged: ____-seven

_____ 16. Where Tucks discovered Winnie's fate

_____ 17. Endless life was a ___ to Angus

_____ 18. It died a natural death

_____ 19. Were stacked up to hide the spring

_____ 20. It explained the cycle of life

Tuck Everlasting Fill In The Blanks 2 Answer Key

SEVENTY	1. Number of years since the jailhouse escape
STUCK	2. How Angus described their situation
BLEW	3. The gallows ___ over in the storm
TOYS	4. Angus and Mae made them to sell: wooden ___
ROWBOAT	5. Winnie went fishing in this
TWENTY	6. Miles's age: ___-two
BABBITT	7. Author
MAE	8. She crawled through the jailhouse window
BLANKET	9. Winnie wrapped up in one to fool the constable
ASH	10. Giant tree in the center of the wood
SPRING	11. It spurted the fountain of youth
SWIM	12. What boys did when they got home
SELL	13. Stranger wanted to do this with the spring water
YEAR	14. Began when the Tucks drank from the spring: live-long ___
EIGHTY	15. Number of years Tucks remained unchanged: ___-seven
CEMETERY	16. Where Tucks discovered Winnie's fate
CURSE	17. Endless life was a ___ to Angus
CAT	18. It died a natural death
PEBBLES	19. Were stacked up to hide the spring
POND	20. It explained the cycle of life

Tuck Everlasting Fill In The Blanks 3

_____ 1. She crawled through the jailhouse window
_____ 2. Stolen by stranger
_____ 3. Winnie wrapped up in one to fool the constable
_____ 4. Grandma thought they made the music
_____ 5. The man in the yellow suit wore a ___ hat
_____ 6. Town near the wood
_____ 7. Time between visits by Tucks' sons: ___ years
_____ 8. Stranger wanted to do this with the spring water
_____ 9. Miles removed it from the jail
_____ 10. Mae's philosophy: ___ day at a time
_____ 11. Began when the Tucks drank from the spring: live-long ___
_____ 12. Became a hero among her peers: ___ Foster
_____ 13. Given in exchange for Winnie's rescue
_____ 14. The gallows ___ over in the storm
_____ 15. Number of years Tucks remained unchanged: ___-seven
_____ 16. Angus and Mae made them to sell: wooden ___
_____ 17. Miles's daughter
_____ 18. Tucks' transportation to Treegap after seventy years
_____ 19. Flashed when the window came out
_____ 20. Miles threw it back because of Winnie: rainbow ___

Tuck Everlasting Fill In The Blanks 3 Answer Key

MAE	1. She crawled through the jailhouse window
HORSE	2. Stolen by stranger
BLANKET	3. Winnie wrapped up in one to fool the constable
ELVES	4. Grandma thought they made the music
BLACK	5. The man in the yellow suit wore a ___ hat
TREEGAP	6. Town near the wood
TEN	7. Time between visits by Tucks' sons: ___ years
SELL	8. Stranger wanted to do this with the spring water
WINDOW	9. Miles removed it from the jail
ONE	10. Mae's philosophy: ___ day at a time
YEAR	11. Began when the Tucks drank from the spring: live-long ___
WINNIE	12. Became a hero among her peers: ___ Foster
WOOD	13. Given in exchange for Winnie's rescue
BLEW	14. The gallows ___ over in the storm
EIGHTY	15. Number of years Tucks remained unchanged: ___-seven
TOYS	16. Angus and Mae made them to sell: wooden ___
ANNA	17. Miles's daughter
BUGGY	18. Tucks' transportation to Treegap after seventy years
LIGHTNING	19. Flashed when the window came out
TROUT	20. Miles threw it back because of Winnie: rainbow ___

Tuck Everlasting Fill In The Blanks 4

_____ 1. Gave a bottle of spring water to Winnie

_____ 2. Where Tucks discovered Winnie's fate

_____ 3. Time between visits by Tucks' sons: ___ years

_____ 4. Mae hit the stranger with this

_____ 5. Became a hero among her peers: ____ Foster

_____ 6. The gallows ___ over in the storm

_____ 7. He arrested Mae

_____ 8. Were stacked up to hide the spring

_____ 9. Miles's age: ___-two

_____ 10. Meeting time for Jesse and Winnie

_____ 11. It died a natural death

_____ 12. Center of universe

_____ 13. Wore a yellow suit

_____ 14. Everlasting amphibian

_____ 15. Color of Tucks' home: ___-red

_____ 16. The man in the yellow suit wore a ___ hat

_____ 17. Endless life was a ___ to Angus

_____ 18. Miles's vocation

_____ 19. Given in exchange for Winnie's rescue

_____ 20. What boys did when they got home

Tuck Everlasting Fill In The Blanks 4 Answer Key

JESSE	1. Gave a bottle of spring water to Winnie
CEMETERY	2. Where Tucks discovered Winnie's fate
TEN	3. Time between visits by Tucks' sons: ___ years
RIFLE	4. Mae hit the stranger with this
WINNIE	5. Became a hero among her peers: ____ Foster
BLEW	6. The gallows ___ over in the storm
CONSTABLE	7. He arrested Mae
PEBBLES	8. Were stacked up to hide the spring
TWENTY	9. Miles's age: ___-two
MIDNIGHT	10. Meeting time for Jesse and Winnie
CAT	11. It died a natural death
WHEEL	12. Center of universe
STRANGER	13. Wore a yellow suit
TOAD	14. Everlasting amphibian
BARN	15. Color of Tucks' home: ___-red
BLACK	16. The man in the yellow suit wore a ___ hat
CURSE	17. Endless life was a ___ to Angus
CARPENTRY	18. Miles's vocation
WOOD	19. Given in exchange for Winnie's rescue
SWIM	20. What boys did when they got home

Tuck Everlasting Matching 1

___ 1. FIREFLIES   A. It spurted the fountain of youth
___ 2. TOAD   B. Given in exchange for Winnie's rescue
___ 3. BLACK   C. Winnie went fishing in this
___ 4. BABBITT   D. Miles's age: ___-two
___ 5. LIGHTNING   E. Grandma thought they made the music
___ 6. BLANKET   F. He hated being stuck in time
___ 7. ANGUS   G. Author
___ 8. SUIT   H. Tucks' transportation to Treegap after seventy years
___ 9. JAIL   I. The man in the yellow suit wore a ___ hat
___ 10. ELVES   J. Month beginning the live-long year
___ 11. CARPENTRY   K. Surrounds touch-me-not cottage: ___ fence
___ 12. SPRING   L. Worn by the stranger: yellow ___
___ 13. WINNIE   M. Letter carved in the ash tree by Angus
___ 14. AUGUST   N. The Foster's cottage: ___-Me-Not
___ 15. KIDNAPPED   O. Tucks did this to Winnie
___ 16. POND   P. Miles's daughter
___ 17. T   Q. He wished to do something important
___ 18. MILES   R. Everlasting amphibian
___ 19. TOUCH   S. Flashed when the window came out
___ 20. IRON   T. Winnie took Mae's place there
___ 21. ANNA   U. It explained the cycle of life
___ 22. BUGGY   V. Became a hero among her peers: ____ Foster
___ 23. WOOD   W. Miles's vocation
___ 24. ROWBOAT   X. Winnie wrapped up in one to fool the constable
___ 25. TWENTY   Y. Winnie liked to catch these

Tuck Everlasting Matching 1 Answer Key

Y -	1. FIREFLIES	A.	It spurted the fountain of youth
R -	2. TOAD	B.	Given in exchange for Winnie's rescue
I -	3. BLACK	C.	Winnie went fishing in this
G -	4. BABBITT	D.	Miles's age: ___-two
S -	5. LIGHTNING	E.	Grandma thought they made the music
X -	6. BLANKET	F.	He hated being stuck in time
F -	7. ANGUS	G.	Author
L -	8. SUIT	H.	Tucks' transportation to Treegap after seventy years
T -	9. JAIL	I.	The man in the yellow suit wore a ___ hat
E -	10. ELVES	J.	Month beginning the live-long year
W -	11. CARPENTRY	K.	Surrounds touch-me-not cottage: ___ fence
A -	12. SPRING	L.	Worn by the stranger: yellow ___
V -	13. WINNIE	M.	Letter carved in the ash tree by Angus
J -	14. AUGUST	N.	The Foster's cottage: ___-Me-Not
O -	15. KIDNAPPED	O.	Tucks did this to Winnie
U -	16. POND	P.	Miles's daughter
M -	17. T	Q.	He wished to do something important
Q -	18. MILES	R.	Everlasting amphibian
N -	19. TOUCH	S.	Flashed when the window came out
K -	20. IRON	T.	Winnie took Mae's place there
P -	21. ANNA	U.	It explained the cycle of life
H -	22. BUGGY	V.	Became a hero among her peers: ____ Foster
B -	23. WOOD	W.	Miles's vocation
C -	24. ROWBOAT	X.	Winnie wrapped up in one to fool the constable
D -	25. TWENTY	Y.	Winnie liked to catch these

Tuck Everlasting Matching 2

___ 1. CEMETERY   A. Where Tucks discovered Winnie's fate
___ 2. WATER   B. It explained the cycle of life
___ 3. KIDNAPPED   C. Center of universe
___ 4. TEN   D. Miles's daughter
___ 5. CONSTABLE   E. Time between visits by Tucks' sons: ___ years
___ 6. TOUCH   F. Were stacked up to hide the spring
___ 7. ANNA   G. He arrested Mae
___ 8. MUSIC   H. Mae's prettiest possession: ___ box
___ 9. ANGUS   I. Meeting time for Jesse and Winnie
___10. BLACK   J. The man in the yellow suit wore a ___ hat
___11. PEBBLES   K. Winnie wrapped up in one to fool the constable
___12. BUGGY   L. Winnie poured bottled ___ over toad.
___13. SELL   M. Number of years since the jailhouse escape
___14. BLANKET   N. The Foster's cottage: ___-Me-Not
___15. BARN   O. Stranger wanted to do this with the spring water
___16. STUCK   P. Tucks' transportation to Treegap after seventy years
___17. MILES   Q. He wished to do something important
___18. SEVENTY   R. Number of years Tucks remained unchanged: ____-seven
___19. BABBITT   S. Jesse's age
___20. EIGHTY   T. Tucks did this to Winnie
___21. POND   U. Author
___22. MIDNIGHT   V. Color of Tucks' home: ___-red
___23. WHEEL   W. How Angus described their situation
___24. SEVENTEEN   X. He hated being stuck in time
___25. WOOD   Y. Given in exchange for Winnie's rescue

Tuck Everlasting Matching 2 Answer Key

- A - 1. CEMETERY
- L - 2. WATER
- T - 3. KIDNAPPED
- E - 4. TEN
- G - 5. CONSTABLE
- N - 6. TOUCH
- D - 7. ANNA
- H - 8. MUSIC
- X - 9. ANGUS
- J - 10. BLACK
- F - 11. PEBBLES
- P - 12. BUGGY
- O - 13. SELL
- K - 14. BLANKET
- V - 15. BARN
- W - 16. STUCK
- Q - 17. MILES
- M - 18. SEVENTY
- U - 19. BABBITT
- R - 20. EIGHTY
- B - 21. POND
- I - 22. MIDNIGHT
- C - 23. WHEEL
- S - 24. SEVENTEEN
- Y - 25. WOOD

A. Where Tucks discovered Winnie's fate
B. It explained the cycle of life
C. Center of universe
D. Miles's daughter
E. Time between visits by Tucks' sons: ___ years
F. Were stacked up to hide the spring
G. He arrested Mae
H. Mae's prettiest possession: ___ box
I. Meeting time for Jesse and Winnie
J. The man in the yellow suit wore a ___ hat
K. Winnie wrapped up in one to fool the constable
L. Winnie poured bottled ___ over toad.
M. Number of years since the jailhouse escape
N. The Foster's cottage: ___-Me-Not
O. Stranger wanted to do this with the spring water
P. Tucks' transportation to Treegap after seventy years
Q. He wished to do something important
R. Number of years Tucks remained unchanged: ___-seven
S. Jesse's age
T. Tucks did this to Winnie
U. Author
V. Color of Tucks' home: ___-red
W. How Angus described their situation
X. He hated being stuck in time
Y. Given in exchange for Winnie's rescue

Tuck Everlasting Matching 3

___ 1. YEAR   A. Began when the Tucks drank from the spring: live-long ____
___ 2. RAIN   B. Color of Tucks' home: ___-red
___ 3. BLEW   C. Worn by the stranger: yellow ___
___ 4. WATER   D. Center of universe
___ 5. BLANKET   E. Began when Mae got out of window
___ 6. TOYS   F. The Foster's cottage: ___-Me-Not
___ 7. WHEEL   G. Winnie poured bottled ___ over toad.
___ 8. NAILS   H. Time between visits by Tucks' sons: ___ years
___ 9. TOAD   I. Miles's age: ___-two
___10. TEN   J. The man in the yellow suit wore a ___ hat
___11. TROUT   K. It explained the cycle of life
___12. TWENTY   L. Flashed when the window came out
___13. SUIT   M. Everlasting amphibian
___14. ANGUS   N. Jesse's age
___15. BLACK   O. Miles removed it from the jail
___16. LIGHTNING   P. Miles removed them from the window
___17. POND   Q. Angus and Mae made them to sell: wooden ___
___18. BARN   R. Stranger wanted to do this with the spring water
___19. JESSE   S. He arrested Mae
___20. SEVENTEEN   T. He hated being stuck in time
___21. CEMETERY   U. The gallows ___ over in the storm
___22. SELL   V. Miles threw it back because of Winnie: rainbow ___
___23. WINDOW   W. Where Tucks discovered Winnie's fate
___24. TOUCH   X. Gave a bottle of spring water to Winnie
___25. CONSTABLE   Y. Winnie wrapped up in one to fool the constable

Tuck Everlasting Matching 3 Answer Key

A - 1. YEAR	A. Began when the Tucks drank from the spring: live-long ___
E - 2. RAIN	B. Color of Tucks' home: ___-red
U - 3. BLEW	C. Worn by the stranger: yellow ___
G - 4. WATER	D. Center of universe
Y - 5. BLANKET	E. Began when Mae got out of window
Q - 6. TOYS	F. The Foster's cottage: ___-Me-Not
D - 7. WHEEL	G. Winnie poured bottled ___ over toad.
P - 8. NAILS	H. Time between visits by Tucks' sons: ___ years
M - 9. TOAD	I. Miles's age: ___-two
H - 10. TEN	J. The man in the yellow suit wore a ___ hat
V - 11. TROUT	K. It explained the cycle of life
I - 12. TWENTY	L. Flashed when the window came out
C - 13. SUIT	M. Everlasting amphibian
T - 14. ANGUS	N. Jesse's age
J - 15. BLACK	O. Miles removed it from the jail
L - 16. LIGHTNING	P. Miles removed them from the window
K - 17. POND	Q. Angus and Mae made them to sell: wooden ___
B - 18. BARN	R. Stranger wanted to do this with the spring water
X - 19. JESSE	S. He arrested Mae
N - 20. SEVENTEEN	T. He hated being stuck in time
W - 21. CEMETERY	U. The gallows ___ over in the storm
R - 22. SELL	V. Miles threw it back because of Winnie: rainbow ___
O - 23. WINDOW	W. Where Tucks discovered Winnie's fate
F - 24. TOUCH	X. Gave a bottle of spring water to Winnie
S - 25. CONSTABLE	Y. Winnie wrapped up in one to fool the constable

Tuck Everlasting Matching 4

___ 1. WINDOW   A. Everlasting amphibian
___ 2. YEAR   B. Meeting time for Jesse and Winnie
___ 3. LIGHTNING   C. Wore a yellow suit
___ 4. CARPENTRY   D. Given in exchange for Winnie's rescue
___ 5. PEBBLES   E. It died a natural death
___ 6. CEMETERY   F. Surrounds touch-me-not cottage: ___ fence
___ 7. DEVIL   G. Miles's wife thought he sold his soul to him
___ 8. WINNIE   H. Mae hit the stranger with this
___ 9. SUIT   I. Miles removed it from the jail
___10. TROUT   J. Miles threw it back because of Winnie: rainbow ___
___11. EIGHTY   K. Where Tucks discovered Winnie's fate
___12. ASH   L. Began when the Tucks drank from the spring: live-long ___
___13. MIDNIGHT   M. Were stacked up to hide the spring
___14. SWIM   N. Angus and Mae made them to sell: wooden ___
___15. POND   O. Worn by the stranger: yellow ___
___16. TOAD   P. Time between visits by Tucks' sons: ___ years
___17. WOOD   Q. Flashed when the window came out
___18. CAT   R. Giant tree in the center of the wood
___19. FOSTERS   S. Number of years Tucks remained unchanged: ___-seven
___20. BABBITT   T. Miles's vocation
___21. TOYS   U. It explained the cycle of life
___22. STRANGER   V. They owned the wood
___23. RIFLE   W. Became a hero among her peers: ___ Foster
___24. IRON   X. What boys did when they got home
___25. TEN   Y. Author

Tuck Everlasting Matching 4 Answer Key

I - 1. WINDOW	A.	Everlasting amphibian
L - 2. YEAR	B.	Meeting time for Jesse and Winnie
Q - 3. LIGHTNING	C.	Wore a yellow suit
T - 4. CARPENTRY	D.	Given in exchange for Winnie's rescue
M - 5. PEBBLES	E.	It died a natural death
K - 6. CEMETERY	F.	Surrounds touch-me-not cottage: ___ fence
G - 7. DEVIL	G.	Miles's wife thought he sold his soul to him
W - 8. WINNIE	H.	Mae hit the stranger with this
O - 9. SUIT	I.	Miles removed it from the jail
J - 10. TROUT	J.	Miles threw it back because of Winnie: rainbow ___
S - 11. EIGHTY	K.	Where Tucks discovered Winnie's fate
R - 12. ASH	L.	Began when the Tucks drank from the spring: live-long ____
B - 13. MIDNIGHT	M.	Were stacked up to hide the spring
X - 14. SWIM	N.	Angus and Mae made them to sell: wooden ___
U - 15. POND	O.	Worn by the stranger: yellow ___
A - 16. TOAD	P.	Time between visits by Tucks' sons: ___ years
D - 17. WOOD	Q.	Flashed when the window came out
E - 18. CAT	R.	Giant tree in the center of the wood
V - 19. FOSTERS	S.	Number of years Tucks remained unchanged: ____-seven
Y - 20. BABBITT	T.	Miles's vocation
N - 21. TOYS	U.	It explained the cycle of life
C - 22. STRANGER	V.	They owned the wood
H - 23. RIFLE	W.	Became a hero among her peers: ____ Foster
F - 24. IRON	X.	What boys did when they got home
P - 25. TEN	Y.	Author

Tuck Everlasting Magic Squares 1

Match the definition with the vocabulary word. Put your answers in the magic squares below. When your answers are correct, all columns and rows will add to the same number.

A. POND
B. WINNIE
C. BABBITT
D. PEBBLES
E. CONSTABLE
F. CARPENTRY
G. TEN
H. DEVIL
I. ROWBOAT
J. ASH
K. SEVENTEEN
L. MAE
M. MIDNIGHT
N. JAIL
O. STRANGER
P. CEMETERY

1. Became a hero among her peers: ____ Foster
2. Time between visits by Tucks' sons: ___ years
3. Jesse's age
4. Winnie took Mae's place there
5. Meeting time for Jesse and Winnie
6. She crawled through the jailhouse window
7. Miles's wife thought he sold his soul to him
8. It explained the cycle of life
9. Where Tucks discovered Winnie's fate
10. Winnie went fishing in this
11. He arrested Mae
12. Were stacked up to hide the spring
13. Author
14. Miles's vocation
15. Giant tree in the center of the wood
16. Wore a yellow suit

A=	B=	C=	D=
E=	F=	G=	H=
I=	J=	K=	L=
M=	N=	O=	P=

Tuck Everlasting Magic Squares 1 Answer Key

Match the definition with the vocabulary word. Put your answers in the magic squares below. When your answers are correct, all columns and rows will add to the same number.

A. POND
B. WINNIE
C. BABBITT
D. PEBBLES
E. CONSTABLE
F. CARPENTRY
G. TEN
H. DEVIL
I. ROWBOAT
J. ASH
K. SEVENTEEN
L. MAE
M. MIDNIGHT
N. JAIL
O. STRANGER
P. CEMETERY

1. Became a hero among her peers: ____ Foster
2. Time between visits by Tucks' sons: ___ years
3. Jesse's age
4. Winnie took Mae's place there
5. Meeting time for Jesse and Winnie
6. She crawled through the jailhouse window
7. Miles's wife thought he sold his soul to him
8. It explained the cycle of life
9. Where Tucks discovered Winnie's fate
10. Winnie went fishing in this
11. He arrested Mae
12. Were stacked up to hide the spring
13. Author
14. Miles's vocation
15. Giant tree in the center of the wood
16. Wore a yellow suit

A=8	B=1	C=13	D=12
E=11	F=14	G=2	H=7
I=10	J=15	K=3	L=6
M=5	N=4	O=16	P=9

Tuck Everlasting Magic Squares 2

Match the definition with the vocabulary word. Put your answers in the magic squares below. When your answers are correct, all columns and rows will add to the same number.

A. TOYS   E. SELL   I. PEBBLES   M. WINDOW
B. BUGGY   F. SPRING   J. TOAD   N. WHEEL
C. CEMETERY   G. KIDNAPPED   K. AUGUST   O. RIFLE
D. ELVES   H. BABBITT   L. MAE   P. BARN

1. It spurted the fountain of youth
2. Were stacked up to hide the spring
3. Mae hit the stranger with this
4. Grandma thought they made the music
5. Miles removed it from the jail
6. Tucks' transportation to Treegap after seventy years
7. Author
8. Month beginning the live-long year
9. Where Tucks discovered Winnie's fate
10. Color of Tucks' home: ___-red
11. Everlasting amphibian
12. Stranger wanted to do this with the spring water
13. She crawled through the jailhouse window
14. Tucks did this to Winnie
15. Angus and Mae made them to sell: wooden ___
16. Center of universe

A=	B=	C=	D=
E=	F=	G=	H=
I=	J=	K=	L=
M=	N=	O=	P=

Tuck Everlasting Magic Squares 2 Answer Key

Match the definition with the vocabulary word. Put your answers in the magic squares below. When your answers are correct, all columns and rows will add to the same number.

A. TOYS
B. BUGGY
C. CEMETERY
D. ELVES
E. SELL
F. SPRING
G. KIDNAPPED
H. BABBITT
I. PEBBLES
J. TOAD
K. AUGUST
L. MAE
M. WINDOW
N. WHEEL
O. RIFLE
P. BARN

1. It spurted the fountain of youth
2. Were stacked up to hide the spring
3. Mae hit the stranger with this
4. Grandma thought they made the music
5. Miles removed it from the jail
6. Tucks' transportation to Treegap after seventy years
7. Author
8. Month beginning the live-long year
9. Where Tucks discovered Winnie's fate
10. Color of Tucks' home: ___-red
11. Everlasting amphibian
12. Stranger wanted to do this with the spring water
13. She crawled through the jailhouse window
14. Tucks did this to Winnie
15. Angus and Mae made them to sell: wooden ___
16. Center of universe

A=15	B=6	C=9	D=4
E=12	F=1	G=14	H=7
I=2	J=11	K=8	L=13
M=5	N=16	O=3	P=10

Tuck Everlasting Magic Squares 3

Match the definition with the vocabulary word. Put your answers in the magic squares below. When your answers are correct, all columns and rows will add to the same number.

A. KIDNAPPED
B. TOAD
C. TOUCH
D. WINNIE
E. BLACK
F. SUIT
G. TOYS
H. IRON
I. ANNA
J. FOSTERS
K. ANGUS
L. WHEEL
M. ELVES
N. AUGUST
O. BUGGY
P. TREEGAP

1. Tucks' transportation to Treegap after seventy years
2. Became a hero among her peers: ____ Foster
3. They owned the wood
4. The man in the yellow suit wore a ____ hat
5. Miles's daughter
6. Worn by the stranger: yellow ____
7. Town near the wood
8. The Foster's cottage: ____-Me-Not
9. Surrounds touch-me-not cottage: ____ fence
10. He hated being stuck in time
11. Tucks did this to Winnie
12. Month beginning the live-long year
13. Everlasting amphibian
14. Grandma thought they made the music
15. Angus and Mae made them to sell: wooden ____
16. Center of universe

A=	B=	C=	D=
E=	F=	G=	H=
I=	J=	K=	L=
M=	N=	O=	P=

26
Copyrighted

Tuck Everlasting Magic Squares 3 Answer Key

Match the definition with the vocabulary word. Put your answers in the magic squares below. When your answers are correct, all columns and rows will add to the same number.

A. KIDNAPPED
B. TOAD
C. TOUCH
D. WINNIE
E. BLACK
F. SUIT
G. TOYS
H. IRON
I. ANNA
J. FOSTERS
K. ANGUS
L. WHEEL
M. ELVES
N. AUGUST
O. BUGGY
P. TREEGAP

1. Tucks' transportation to Treegap after seventy years
2. Became a hero among her peers: ____ Foster
3. They owned the wood
4. The man in the yellow suit wore a ___ hat
5. Miles's daughter
6. Worn by the stranger: yellow ___
7. Town near the wood
8. The Foster's cottage: ___-Me-Not
9. Surrounds touch-me-not cottage: ___ fence
10. He hated being stuck in time
11. Tucks did this to Winnie
12. Month beginning the live-long year
13. Everlasting amphibian
14. Grandma thought they made the music
15. Angus and Mae made them to sell: wooden ___
16. Center of universe

A=11	B=13	C=8	D=2
E=4	F=6	G=15	H=9
I=5	J=3	K=10	L=16
M=14	N=12	O=1	P=7

Tuck Everlasting Magic Squares 4

Match the definition with the vocabulary word. Put your answers in the magic squares below. When your answers are correct, all columns and rows will add to the same number.

A. IRON
B. WOOD
C. NAILS
D. SWIM
E. MAE
F. MUSIC
G. CONSTABLE
H. WINDOW
I. TREEGAP
J. FIREFLIES
K. ROWBOAT
L. RIFLE
M. KIDNAPPED
N. SPRING
O. SUIT
P. HORSE

1. Miles removed it from the jail
2. Tucks did this to Winnie
3. Given in exchange for Winnie's rescue
4. Winnie went fishing in this
5. Winnie liked to catch these
6. Miles removed them from the window
7. Stolen by stranger
8. She crawled through the jailhouse window
9. Worn by the stranger: yellow ___
10. Mae's prettiest possession: ___ box
11. Town near the wood
12. What boys did when they got home
13. Surrounds touch-me-not cottage: ___ fence
14. Mae hit the stranger with this
15. He arrested Mae
16. It spurted the fountain of youth

A=	B=	C=	D=
E=	F=	G=	H=
I=	J=	K=	L=
M=	N=	O=	P=

Tuck Everlasting Magic Squares 4 Answer Key

Match the definition with the vocabulary word. Put your answers in the magic squares below. When your answers are correct, all columns and rows will add to the same number.

A. IRON
B. WOOD
C. NAILS
D. SWIM
E. MAE
F. MUSIC
G. CONSTABLE
H. WINDOW
I. TREEGAP
J. FIREFLIES
K. ROWBOAT
L. RIFLE
M. KIDNAPPED
N. SPRING
O. SUIT
P. HORSE

1. Miles removed it from the jail
2. Tucks did this to Winnie
3. Given in exchange for Winnie's rescue
4. Winnie went fishing in this
5. Winnie liked to catch these
6. Miles removed them from the window
7. Stolen by stranger
8. She crawled through the jailhouse window
9. Worn by the stranger: yellow ___
10. Mae's prettiest possession: ___ box
11. Town near the wood
12. What boys did when they got home
13. Surrounds touch-me-not cottage: ___ fence
14. Mae hit the stranger with this
15. He arrested Mae
16. It spurted the fountain of youth

A=13	B=3	C=6	D=12
E=8	F=10	G=15	H=1
I=11	J=5	K=4	L=14
M=2	N=16	O=9	P=7

Tuck Everlasting Word Search 1

```
P O N D B S T R A N G E R G M S O N E M
Q N F M C U B R H S W S M J U W W F V S
C E V Z K C G A O R E I S G S I J J M P
J E G G F K R G B U C V N R I M D H E Q
S T U C K G I G Y B T B E D C B L A C K
E N L D Y T F X G C I P L N O W M A Z F
I E W T N K L B N M B T J A T W R U J X
L V Y J Z A E M I H F F T J N Y W G E T
F E B E Q X I T R E E G A P W K S U S C
E S K J A V I L P T O U C H E F E S S S
R H V C U R S E S A D J A I L W A T E R
I O T Q O G K R N G S V G I B Q A O C T
F R O N D T E N Y Y C H V J S O J A D G
T S Y C B T A P T A T E Z T B C Z D R N
C E S S S R A I N Y D S M W B A R N W W
C V N O E V V G E K U Z O I W T W H J J
R L F Z H L U B W I D R Z P L O E F Z Q
W E R W C S L T T W I N N I E E O Z R P
V L V G Z P E B B L E S W S L S S D Y V
```

Angus and Mae made them to sell: wooden ___ (4)
Author (7)
Became a hero among her peers: ____ Foster (6)
Began when Mae got out of window (4)
Began when the Tucks drank from the spring: live-long ____ (4)
Center of universe (5)
Color of Tucks' home: ___-red (4)
Endless life was a ___ to Angus (5)
Everlasting amphibian (4)
Gave a bottle of spring water to Winnie (5)
Giant tree in the center of the wood (3)
Given in exchange for Winnie's rescue (4)
Grandma thought they made the music (5)
He hated being stuck in time (5)
He wished to do something important (5)
How Angus described their situation (5)
It died a natural death (3)
It explained the cycle of life (4)
It spurted the fountain of youth (6)
Jesse's age (9)
Mae hit the stranger with this (5)
Mae's philosophy: ___ day at a time (3)
Mae's prettiest possession: ___ box (5)
Miles removed it from the jail (6)
Miles removed them from the window (5)
Miles threw it back because of Winnie: rainbow ___ (5)
Miles's age: ___-two (6)
Miles's daughter (4)
Miles's wife thought he sold his soul to him (5)
Month beginning the live-long year (6)
Number of years Tucks remained unchanged: ____-seven (6)
Number of years since the jailhouse escape (7)
She crawled through the jailhouse window (3)
Stolen by stranger (5)
Stranger wanted to do this with the spring water (4)
Surrounds touch-me-not cottage: ___ fence (4)
The Foster's cottage: ___-Me-Not (5)
The gallows ___ over in the storm (4)
The man in the yellow suit wore a ___ hat (5)
They owned the wood (7)
Time between visits by Tucks' sons: ___ years (3)
Town near the wood (7)
Tucks' transportation to Treegap after seventy years (5)
Were stacked up to hide the spring (7)
What boys did when they got home (4)
Winnie liked to catch these (9)
Winnie poured bottled ___ over toad. (5)
Winnie took Mae's place there (4)
Winnie went fishing in this (7)
Winnie wrapped up in one to fool the constable (7)
Wore a yellow suit (8)
Worn by the stranger: yellow ___ (4)

Tuck Everlasting Word Search 1 Answer Key

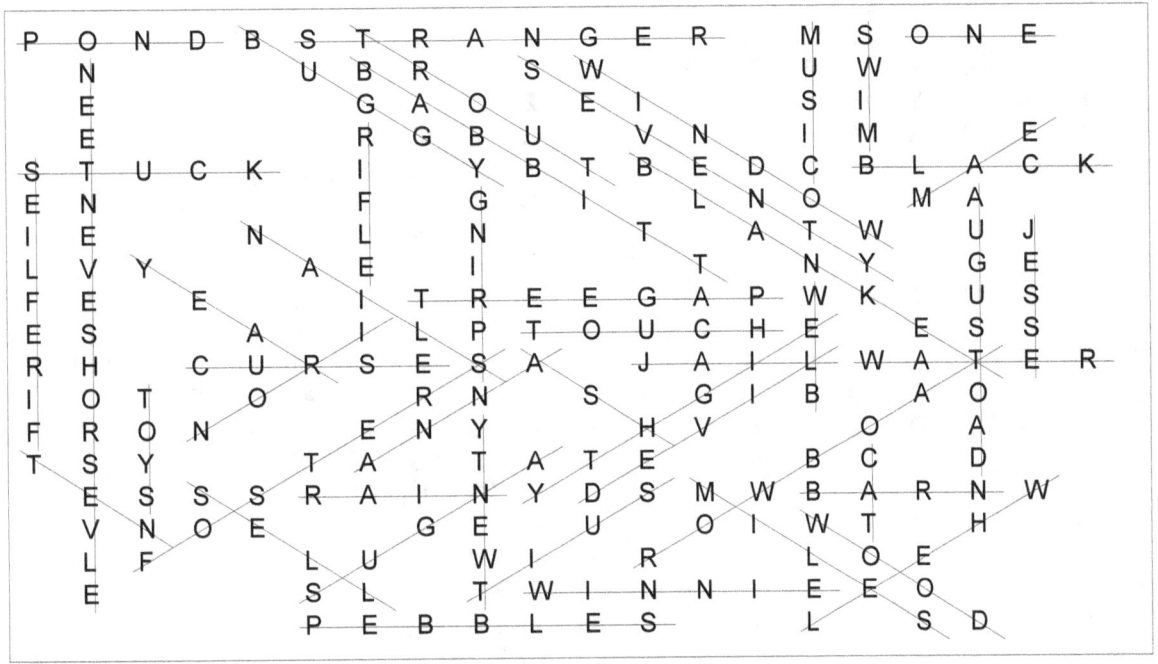

Angus and Mae made them to sell: wooden ___ (4)
Author (7)
Became a hero among her peers: ____ Foster (6)
Began when Mae got out of window (4)
Began when the Tucks drank from the spring: live-long ____ (4)
Center of universe (5)
Color of Tucks' home: ___-red (4)
Endless life was a ___ to Angus (5)
Everlasting amphibian (4)
Gave a bottle of spring water to Winnie (5)
Giant tree in the center of the wood (3)
Given in exchange for Winnie's rescue (4)
Grandma thought they made the music (5)
He hated being stuck in time (5)
He wished to do something important (5)
How Angus described their situation (5)
It died a natural death (3)
It explained the cycle of life (4)
It spurted the fountain of youth (6)
Jesse's age (9)
Mae hit the stranger with this (5)
Mae's philosophy: ___ day at a time (3)
Mae's prettiest possession: ___ box (5)
Miles removed it from the jail (6)
Miles removed them from the window (5)
Miles threw it back because of Winnie: rainbow ___ (5)

Miles's age: ___-two (6)
Miles's daughter (4)
Miles's wife thought he sold his soul to him (5)
Month beginning the live-long year (6)
Number of years Tucks remained unchanged: ____-seven (6)
Number of years since the jailhouse escape (7)
She crawled through the jailhouse window (3)
Stolen by stranger (5)
Stranger wanted to do this with the spring water (4)
Surrounds touch-me-not cottage: ___ fence (4)
The Foster's cottage: ___-Me-Not (5)
The gallows ___ over in the storm (4)
The man in the yellow suit wore a ___ hat (5)
They owned the wood (7)
Time between visits by Tucks' sons: ___ years (3)
Town near the wood (7)
Tucks' transportation to Treegap after seventy years (5)
Were stacked up to hide the spring (7)
What boys did when they got home (4)
Winnie liked to catch these (9)
Winnie poured bottled ___ over toad. (5)
Winnie took Mae's place there (4)
Winnie went fishing in this (7)
Winnie wrapped up in one to fool the constable (7)
Wore a yellow suit (8)
Worn by the stranger: yellow ___ (4)

Tuck Everlasting Word Search 2

```
W T B M G Z E S R U C Z D F R J E S S E
O W A Z A F T T Q X Q F E W M I R B C P
O E B N Y E W U R Z L Z V P Z E F G E W
D N B B N M N C W E T Q I L T W V L M Z
L T I T O A D K B U E C L S P O N D E F
B Y T T A O B W O R H G O C Z D L W T Y
H F T S L Y X R K W X F A K Z N M G E D
C I L G T S T T T M I F G P H I C Y R R
Q R I H W R G T T Y N N K X O W I Y Y S
S E G N W R A H S N M J N W R R T T S M
Z F H P M T G N U Z R V A I S S O K I M
S L T S P R I N G Y T H G I E A N G U S
E I N N D Q S S U E D H G G L A N S S Z
L E I T C R E E A O R A B G I W I Y R C
B S N R S W V V L N T L S L M C A O A S
B U G G Y B L E W E L O S H A B R T Y D
E A T L V G E N B E V W U Y W C E Y E K
P J R X M H D T S Y I K P C Y N K K A R
R N J N W S N Y P M G R F C H X V R R T
```

Angus and Mae made them to sell: wooden ___ (4)
Author (7)
Became a hero among her peers: ____ Foster (6)
Began when Mae got out of window (4)
Began when the Tucks drank from the spring: live-long ____ (4)
Center of universe (5)
Color of Tucks' home: ___-red (4)
Endless life was a ____ to Angus (5)
Everlasting amphibian (4)
Flashed when the window came out (9)
Gave a bottle of spring water to Winnie (5)
Giant tree in the center of the wood (3)
Given in exchange for Winnie's rescue (4)
Grandma thought they made the music (5)
He hated being stuck in time (5)
He wished to do something important (5)
How Angus described their situation (5)
It died a natural death (3)
It explained the cycle of life (4)
It spurted the fountain of youth (6)
Mae hit the stranger with this (5)
Mae's philosophy: ___ day at a time (3)
Mae's prettiest possession: ___ box (5)
Miles removed it from the jail (6)
Miles removed them from the window (5)
Miles threw it back because of Winnie: rainbow ___ (5)

Miles's age: ___-two (6)
Miles's daughter (4)
Miles's wife thought he sold his soul to him (5)
Month beginning the live-long year (6)
Number of years Tucks remained unchanged: ____-seven (6)
Number of years since the jailhouse escape (7)
She crawled through the jailhouse window (3)
Stolen by stranger (5)
Stranger wanted to do this with the spring water (4)
Surrounds touch-me-not cottage: ___ fence (4)
The Foster's cottage: ___-Me-Not (5)
The gallows ___ over in the storm (4)
The man in the yellow suit wore a ___ hat (5)
They owned the wood (7)
Time between visits by Tucks' sons: ___ years (3)
Town near the wood (7)
Tucks' transportation to Treegap after seventy years (5)
Were stacked up to hide the spring (7)
What boys did when they got home (4)
Where Tucks discovered Winnie's fate (8)
Winnie liked to catch these (9)
Winnie poured bottled ___ over toad. (5)
Winnie took Mae's place there (4)
Winnie went fishing in this (7)
Wore a yellow suit (8)
Worn by the stranger: yellow ___ (4)

Tuck Everlasting Word Search 2 Answer Key

- Angus and Mae made them to sell: wooden ___ (4)
- Author (7)
- Became a hero among her peers: ____ Foster (6)
- Began when Mae got out of window (4)
- Began when the Tucks drank from the spring: live-long ____ (4)
- Center of universe (5)
- Color of Tucks' home: ___-red (4)
- Endless life was a ___ to Angus (5)
- Everlasting amphibian (4)
- Flashed when the window came out (9)
- Gave a bottle of spring water to Winnie (5)
- Giant tree in the center of the wood (3)
- Given in exchange for Winnie's rescue (4)
- Grandma thought they made the music (5)
- He hated being stuck in time (5)
- He wished to do something important (5)
- How Angus described their situation (5)
- It died a natural death (3)
- It explained the cycle of life (4)
- It spurted the fountain of youth (6)
- Mae hit the stranger with this (5)
- Mae's philosophy: ___ day at a time (3)
- Mae's prettiest possession: ___ box (5)
- Miles removed it from the jail (6)
- Miles removed them from the window (5)
- Miles threw it back because of Winnie: rainbow ___ (5)
- Miles's age: ___-two (6)
- Miles's daughter (4)
- Miles's wife thought he sold his soul to him (5)
- Month beginning the live-long year (6)
- Number of years Tucks remained unchanged: ____-seven (6)
- Number of years since the jailhouse escape (7)
- She crawled through the jailhouse window (3)
- Stolen by stranger (5)
- Stranger wanted to do this with the spring water (4)
- Surrounds touch-me-not cottage: ___ fence (4)
- The Foster's cottage: ___-Me-Not (5)
- The gallows ___ over in the storm (4)
- The man in the yellow suit wore a ___ hat (5)
- They owned the wood (7)
- Time between visits by Tucks' sons: ___ years (3)
- Town near the wood (7)
- Tucks' transportation to Treegap after seventy years (5)
- Were stacked up to hide the spring (7)
- What boys did when they got home (4)
- Where Tucks discovered Winnie's fate (8)
- Winnie liked to catch these (9)
- Winnie poured bottled ___ over toad. (5)
- Winnie took Mae's place there (4)
- Winnie went fishing in this (7)
- Wore a yellow suit (8)
- Worn by the stranger: yellow ___ (4)

Tuck Everlasting Word Search 3

```
B U G G Y R G T K A C A T P P S B A R N
L L S E R E V O I R U E N O R E S N T Z
E F A B T T Y T I S K G J N J V P G P D
W R T X N A Y F D N P T U D A E R U E M
I Y T N E W T C N M H R S E N I S B B V
N P I M P K X H A Z U W J I T G L B G W
D V B B R J B Q P K S S H N F Y A P L J
O B B N A B E R E R T Z I E D L J E M
W L A D C X J S D K R D Q C E G R S V J
G Q B F S V E D S B A L H T E O F Y M D
F B X E B L T D E E N G S E T W I R F W
H J V L L V F L N B G G R C B M Q E O T
N L I V E D B H W L E T R O U T A E S D
E C L J S A H S I A R Y A V W I I F T M
L X N L T P T E N C T T K J N G D L T V
T M I S E D D L N K M C T S H J A I E Z
W A N R N O Q I I A U W O T W A O R H
N O T E O C E M E T E R R S S U I T S Y
C M T W V N W F S C U R S E C L M A Y X
```

ANGUS	CAT	JAIL	RIFLE	TOUCH
ANNA	CEMETERY	JESSE	ROWBOAT	TOYS
ASH	CONSTABLE	KIDNAPPED	SELL	TREEGAP
AUGUST	CURSE	MAE	SEVENTY	TROUT
BABBITT	DEVIL	MILES	SPRING	TWENTY
BARN	EIGHTY	MUSIC	STRANGER	WATER
BLACK	ELVES	NAILS	STUCK	WHEEL
BLANKET	FIREFLIES	ONE	SUIT	WINDOW
BLEW	FOSTERS	PEBBLES	SWIM	WINNIE
BUGGY	HORSE	POND	TEN	WOOD
CARPENTRY	IRON	RAIN	TOAD	YEAR

Tuck Everlasting Word Search 3 Answer Key

ANGUS	CAT	JAIL	RIFLE	TOUCH
ANNA	CEMETERY	JESSE	ROWBOAT	TOYS
ASH	CONSTABLE	KIDNAPPED	SELL	TREEGAP
AUGUST	CURSE	MAE	SEVENTY	TROUT
BABBITT	DEVIL	MILES	SPRING	TWENTY
BARN	EIGHTY	MUSIC	STRANGER	WATER
BLACK	ELVES	NAILS	STUCK	WHEEL
BLANKET	FIREFLIES	ONE	SUIT	WINDOW
BLEW	FOSTERS	PEBBLES	SWIM	WINNIE
BUGGY	HORSE	POND	TEN	WOOD
CARPENTRY	IRON	RAIN	TOAD	YEAR

Tuck Everlasting Word Search 4

```
R S C B T F I R E F L I E S R E T S O F
O X D E S O S P D C O N S T A B E K R S
W E D R M U U P A G E E R T Y L L V E E
B I R J L E T C Z C B A H N T H C U S P
O N S R I Z T E H B P U O H V G T R W L
A N S M V C T E N M R G B G I M J A S P
T I I X E Y N S R T Y U P L E L A T I N
M W O O D N O P D Y Y S E V E N T R L P
S Q E M D R K S M G T I H C W N G R S N
Z G W N F Q U X G U L X B M A N Y A B L
A G M I T G Y C Y R W R I P E D A R O K
S L I A N Y B C A L B T F E L A N O C C
H P B A I D R C V K V B E L M A N W T T
M T R V A R O S A K L S L B K M E S A A
F W E I R K O W T T I B B A B J E S L L
K L C N N K G N L I D L G N N L M C E E
M I D N I G H T T U E G K X L K F Y Y Y
L G H C T N I P N S R I F L E G E O F J
N W J C A R P E N T R Y J T R O U T D C
```

ANGUS CEMETERY LIGHTNING SELL TREEGAP
ANNA CONSTABLE MAE SEVENTEEN TROUT
ASH CURSE MIDNIGHT SEVENTY TWENTY
AUGUST DEVIL MILES SPRING WATER
BABBITT EIGHTY MUSIC STRANGER WHEEL
BARN ELVES NAILS STUCK WINDOW
BLACK FIREFLIES ONE SUIT WINNIE
BLANKET FOSTERS PEBBLES SWIM WOOD
BLEW HORSE POND TEN YEAR
BUGGY IRON RAIN TOAD
CARPENTRY JAIL RIFLE TOUCH
CAT JESSE ROWBOAT TOYS

Tuck Everlasting Word Search 4 Answer Key

ANGUS	CEMETERY	LIGHTNING	SELL	TREEGAP
ANNA	CONSTABLE	MAE	SEVENTEEN	TROUT
ASH	CURSE	MIDNIGHT	SEVENTY	TWENTY
AUGUST	DEVIL	MILES	SPRING	WATER
BABBITT	EIGHTY	MUSIC	STRANGER	WHEEL
BARN	ELVES	NAILS	STUCK	WINDOW
BLACK	FIREFLIES	ONE	SUIT	WINNIE
BLANKET	FOSTERS	PEBBLES	SWIM	WOOD
BLEW	HORSE	POND	TEN	YEAR
BUGGY	IRON	RAIN	TOAD	
CARPENTRY	JAIL	RIFLE	TOUCH	
CAT	JESSE	ROWBOAT	TOYS	

Tuck Everlasting Crossword 1

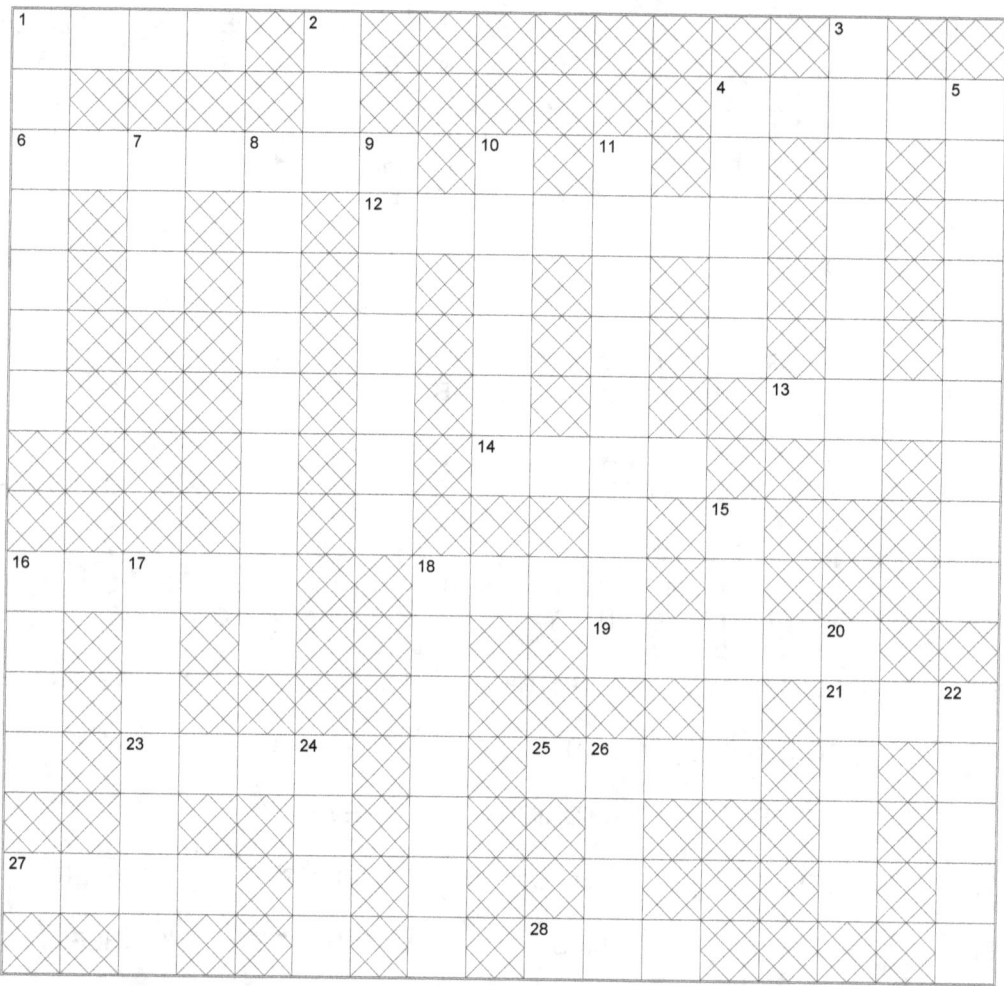

Across
1. It explained the cycle of life
4. Center of universe
6. Winnie wrapped up in one to fool the constable
12. Winnie went fishing in this
13. Surrounds touch-me-not cottage: ___ fence
14. Began when the Tucks drank from the spring: live-long ____
16. Mae hit the stranger with this
18. Stranger wanted to do this with the spring water
19. Grandma thought they made the music
21. Time between visits by Tucks' sons: ___ years
23. Angus and Mae made them to sell: wooden ___
25. Winnie took Mae's place there
27. Color of Tucks' home: ___-red
28. She crawled through the jailhouse window

Down
1. Were stacked up to hide the spring
2. Mae's philosophy: ___ day at a time
3. Where Tucks discovered Winnie's fate
4. Winnie poured bottled ___ over toad.
5. Flashed when the window came out
7. Giant tree in the center of the wood
8. Tucks did this to Winnie
9. Town near the wood
10. Miles's age: ___-two
11. He arrested Mae
15. Miles's wife thought he sold his soul to him
16. Began when Mae got out of window
17. They owned the wood
18. Number of years since the jailhouse escape
20. How Angus described their situation
22. Miles removed them from the window
24. Worn by the stranger: yellow ___
26. Miles's daughter

Tuck Everlasting Crossword 1 Answer Key

	1 P	O	N	D		2 O						3 C		
	E					N				4 W	H	E	E	5 L
	6 B	7 L	8 A	N	9 K	E	10 T		11 C	A		M		I
	B		S		I		12 R	O	W	B	O	A	T	
	L		H		I		D			E		T		G
	L		H		D		E			O		T		H
	E				N		E			N		E		T
	S				A		G		T			13 I	R	O	N
					P		A		14 Y	E	A	R		Y		I
					P		P		B			15 D			N
	16 R	17 I	F	L	E		18 S	E	L	L		E			G
	A		O		D		E		19 E	L	V	E	S	20 S	
	I		S				V			I			21 T	E	22 N
				23 T	O	Y	24 S		25 J	26 A	I	L		U		A
	N		E				U		E		N			C		I
	27 B	A	R	N		I		T		N			K		L
			S			T		Y		28 M	A	E			S

Across
1. It explained the cycle of life
4. Center of universe
6. Winnie wrapped up in one to fool the constable
12. Winnie went fishing in this
13. Surrounds touch-me-not cottage: ___ fence
14. Began when the Tucks drank from the spring: live-long ___
16. Mae hit the stranger with this
18. Stranger wanted to do this with the spring water
19. Grandma thought they made the music
21. Time between visits by Tucks' sons: ___ years
23. Angus and Mae made them to sell: wooden ___
25. Winnie took Mae's place there
27. Color of Tucks' home: ___-red
28. She crawled through the jailhouse window

Down
1. Were stacked up to hide the spring
2. Mae's philosophy: ___ day at a time
3. Where Tucks discovered Winnie's fate
4. Winnie poured bottled ___ over toad.
5. Flashed when the window came out
7. Giant tree in the center of the wood
8. Tucks did this to Winnie
9. Town near the wood
10. Miles's age: ___-two
11. He arrested Mae
15. Miles's wife thought he sold his soul to him
16. Began when Mae got out of window
17. They owned the wood
18. Number of years since the jailhouse escape
20. How Angus described their situation
22. Miles removed them from the window
24. Worn by the stranger: yellow ___
26. Miles's daughter

Tuck Everlasting Crossword 2

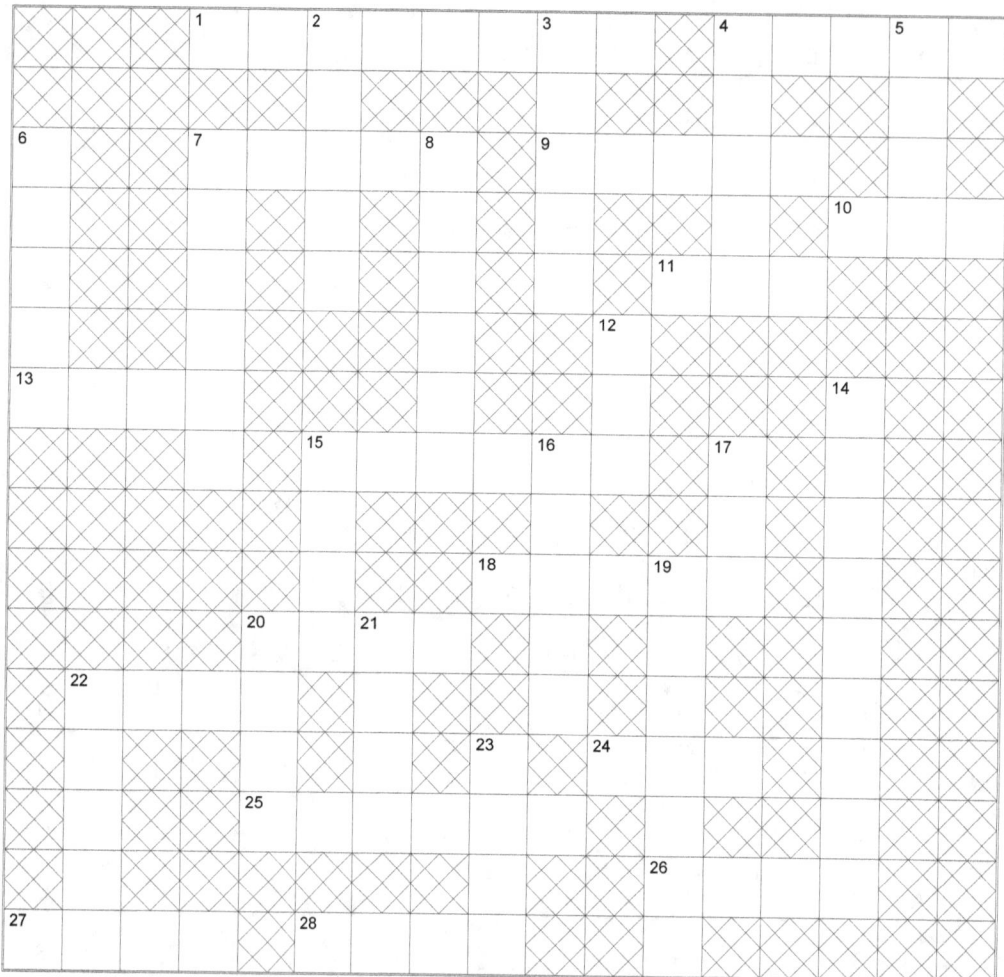

Across
1. Meeting time for Jesse and Winnie
4. Mae's prettiest possession: ___ box
7. Grandma thought they made the music
9. Mae hit the stranger with this
10. Mae's philosophy: ___ day at a time
11. Giant tree in the center of the wood
13. Worn by the stranger: yellow ___
15. Month beginning the live-long year
18. Endless life was a ___ to Angus
20. Color of Tucks' home: ___-red
22. Winnie took Mae's place there
24. Time between visits by Tucks' sons: ___ years
25. Miles removed it from the jail
26. Everlasting amphibian
27. Stranger wanted to do this with the spring water
28. Given in exchange for Winnie's rescue

Down
2. Miles's wife thought he sold his soul to him
3. Stolen by stranger
4. He wished to do something important
5. Surrounds touch-me-not cottage: ___ fence
6. He hated being stuck in time
7. Number of years Tucks remained unchanged: ____-seven
8. It spurted the fountain of youth
12. It died a natural death
14. Tucks did this to Winnie
15. Miles's daughter
16. How Angus described their situation
17. She crawled through the jailhouse window
19. Number of years since the jailhouse escape
20. The gallows ___ over in the storm
21. Began when Mae got out of window
22. Gave a bottle of spring water to Winnie
23. It explained the cycle of life

Tuck Everlasting Crossword 2 Answer Key

			1 M	I	2 D	N	I	3 G	H	T		4 M	U	S	5 I	C
					E			O				I			R	
6 A		7 E	L	V	8 E	S		9 R	I	F	L	E			O	
N		I			P			S				E		10 O	N	E
G		G			R			E			11 A	S	H			
U		H			I					12 C						
13 S	U	I	T		N					A				14 K		
		Y		15 A	U	G	U	16 S	T			17 M		I		
				N				T				A		D		
				N			18 C	U	R	19 S	E		N			
			20 B	A	21 R	N		C		E				A		
	22 J	A	I	L		A		K		V				P		
	E			E		I		23 P		24 T	E	N		P		
	S		25 W	I	N	D	O	W		N				E		
	S							N		26 T	O	A	D			
27 S	E	L	L		28 W	O	O	D		Y						

Across
1. Meeting time for Jesse and Winnie
4. Mae's prettiest possession: ___ box
7. Grandma thought they made the music
9. Mae hit the stranger with this
10. Mae's philosophy: ___ day at a time
11. Giant tree in the center of the wood
13. Worn by the stranger: yellow ___
15. Month beginning the live-long year
18. Endless life was a ___ to Angus
20. Color of Tucks' home: ___-red
22. Winnie took Mae's place there
24. Time between visits by Tucks' sons: ___ years
25. Miles removed it from the jail
26. Everlasting amphibian
27. Stranger wanted to do this with the spring water
28. Given in exchange for Winnie's rescue

Down
2. Miles's wife thought he sold his soul to him
3. Stolen by stranger
4. He wished to do something important
5. Surrounds touch-me-not cottage: ___ fence
6. He hated being stuck in time
7. Number of years Tucks remained unchanged: ____-seven
8. It spurted the fountain of youth
12. It died a natural death
14. Tucks did this to Winnie
15. Miles's daughter
16. How Angus described their situation
17. She crawled through the jailhouse window
19. Number of years since the jailhouse escape
20. The gallows ___ over in the storm
21. Began when Mae got out of window
22. Gave a bottle of spring water to Winnie
23. It explained the cycle of life

Tuck Everlasting Crossword 3

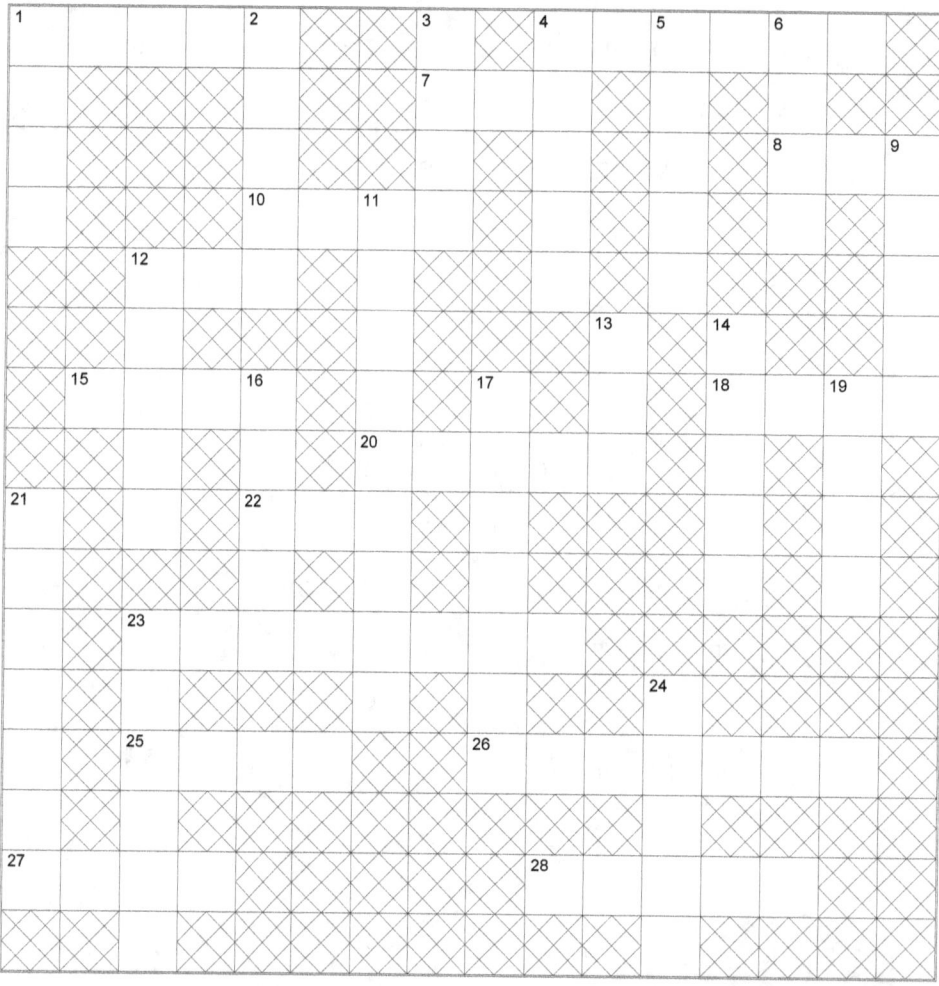

Across
1. The Foster's cottage: ___-Me-Not
4. Became a hero among her peers: ____ Foster
7. Giant tree in the center of the wood
8. Mae's philosophy: ___ day at a time
10. Stranger wanted to do this with the spring water
12. She crawled through the jailhouse window
15. The gallows ___ over in the storm
18. Angus and Mae made them to sell: wooden ___
20. Miles threw it back because of Winnie: rainbow ___
22. Time between visits by Tucks' sons: ___ years
23. Wore a yellow suit
25. Began when Mae got out of window
26. Number of years since the jailhouse escape
27. It explained the cycle of life
28. Mae's prettiest possession: ___ box

Down
1. Everlasting amphibian
2. Stolen by stranger
3. Winnie took Mae's place there
4. Center of universe
5. Miles removed them from the window
6. Surrounds touch-me-not cottage: ___ fence
9. Grandma thought they made the music
11. Flashed when the window came out
12. He wished to do something important
13. It died a natural death
14. How Angus described their situation
16. Winnie poured bottled ___ over toad.
17. They owned the wood
19. Began when the Tucks drank from the spring: live-long ___
21. Town near the wood
23. It spurted the fountain of youth
24. Gave a bottle of spring water to Winnie

Tuck Everlasting Crossword 3 Answer Key

	1 T	O	U	C	2 H		3 J		4 W	I	5 N	N	6 I	E	
	O				O		7 A	S	H	E	A		R		
	A				R		I		E		I		8 O	N	9 E
	D			10 S	E	11 L	L		E		L		N		L
			12 M	A	E	I			L		S				V
			I			G			13 C		14 S				E
		15 B	L	E	16 W	H		17 F	A		18 T	O	19 Y	S
			E		A	20 T	R	O	U	T	U		E		
	21 T		S		22 T	E	N		S		C		A		
	R				E	I			T		K		R		
	E		23 S	T	R	A	N	G	E	R					
	E		P			G			R		24 J				
	25 G	R	A	I	N			26 S	E	V	E	N	T	Y	
	A		I								S				
	27 P	O	N	D				28 M	U	S	I	C			
			G								E				

Across
1. The Foster's cottage: ___-Me-Not
4. Became a hero among her peers: ____ Foster
7. Giant tree in the center of the wood
8. Mae's philosophy: ___ day at a time
10. Stranger wanted to do this with the spring water
12. She crawled through the jailhouse window
15. The gallows ___ over in the storm
18. Angus and Mae made them to sell: wooden ___
20. Miles threw it back because of Winnie: rainbow ___
22. Time between visits by Tucks' sons: ___ years
23. Wore a yellow suit
25. Began when Mae got out of window
26. Number of years since the jailhouse escape
27. It explained the cycle of life
28. Mae's prettiest possession: ___ box

Down
1. Everlasting amphibian
2. Stolen by stranger
3. Winnie took Mae's place there
4. Center of universe
5. Miles removed them from the window
6. Surrounds touch-me-not cottage: ___ fence
9. Grandma thought they made the music
11. Flashed when the window came out
12. He wished to do something important
13. It died a natural death
14. How Angus described their situation
16. Winnie poured bottled ___ over toad.
17. They owned the wood
19. Began when the Tucks drank from the spring: live-long ____
21. Town near the wood
23. It spurted the fountain of youth
24. Gave a bottle of spring water to Winnie

Tuck Everlasting Crossword 4

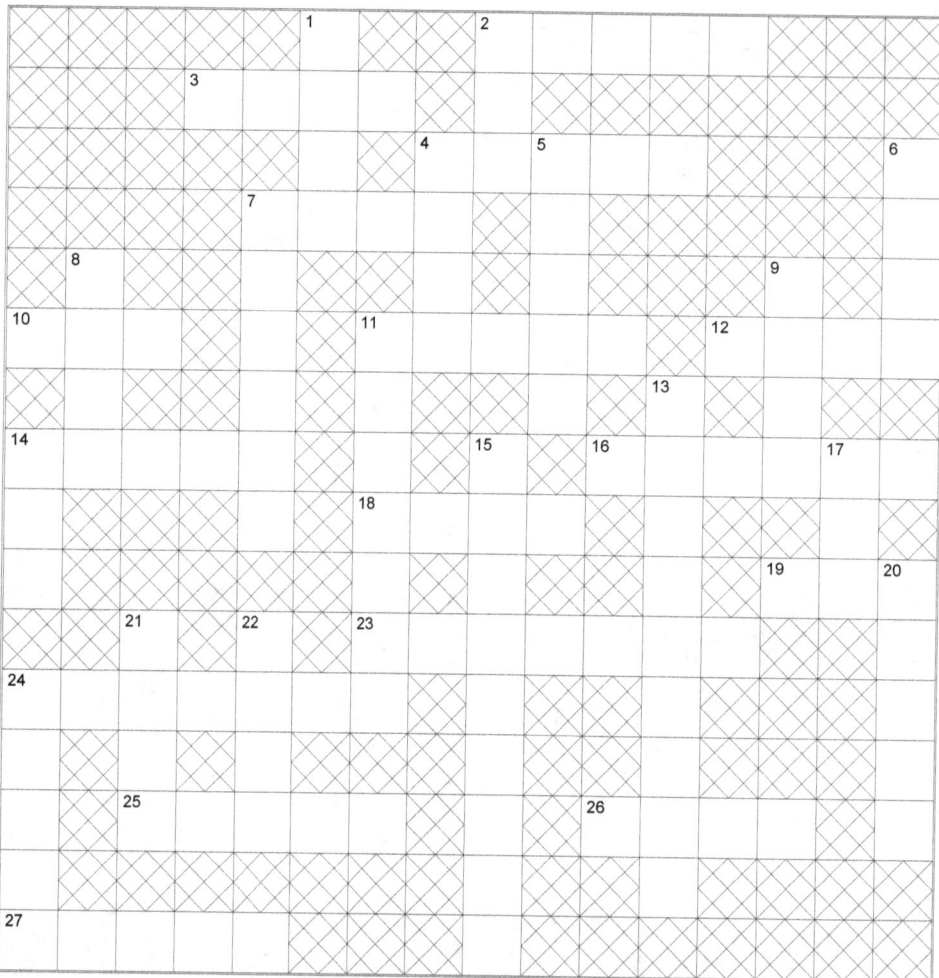

Across
2. He wished to do something important
3. Began when the Tucks drank from the spring: live-long ___
4. Gave a bottle of spring water to Winnie
7. Miles's daughter
10. It died a natural death
11. The man in the yellow suit wore a ___ hat
12. It explained the cycle of life
14. He hated being stuck in time
16. Miles removed it from the jail
18. The gallows ___ over in the storm
19. Time between visits by Tucks' sons: ___ years
23. Town near the wood
24. Winnie went fishing in this
25. Mae's prettiest possession: ___ box
26. Stranger wanted to do this with the spring water
27. Grandma thought they made the music

Down
1. Color of Tucks' home: ___-red
2. She crawled through the jailhouse window
4. Winnie took Mae's place there
5. How Angus described their situation
6. Everlasting amphibian
7. Month beginning the live-long year
8. Began when Mae got out of window
9. Given in exchange for Winnie's rescue
11. Author
13. Tucks did this to Winnie
14. Giant tree in the center of the wood
15. Jesse's age
17. Mae's philosophy: ___ day at a time
20. Miles removed them from the window
21. What boys did when they got home
22. Angus and Mae made them to sell: wooden ___
24. Mae hit the stranger with this

Tuck Everlasting Crossword 4 Answer Key

					1 B		2 M	I	L	E	S		
		3 Y	E	A	R		A						
					R	4	5 S	S	E				6 T
			7 A	N	N	A		T					O
	8 R		U			I		U			9 W		A
10 C	A	T		11 G		B	L	A	C	12 P	O	N	D
	I			U		A		K	13 K	O			
14 A	N	G	U	S		15 B	16 W	I	N	D	17 O	W	
S				T		18 B	L	E	W		N		
H						I		V		N	19 T	E	20 N
		21 S		22 T	23 T	R	E	E	G	A	P		A
24 R	O	W	B	O	A	T		N		P			I
I		I		Y		T		P					L
F		25 M	U	S	I	C		26 S	E	L	L		S
L						E		D					
27 E	L	V	E	S		N							

Across
2. He wished to do something important
3. Began when the Tucks drank from the spring: live-long ___
4. Gave a bottle of spring water to Winnie
7. Miles's daughter
10. It died a natural death
11. The man in the yellow suit wore a ___ hat
12. It explained the cycle of life
14. He hated being stuck in time
16. Miles removed it from the jail
18. The gallows ___ over in the storm
19. Time between visits by Tucks' sons: ___ years
23. Town near the wood
24. Winnie went fishing in this
25. Mae's prettiest possession: ___ box
26. Stranger wanted to do this with the spring water
27. Grandma thought they made the music

Down
1. Color of Tucks' home: ___-red
2. She crawled through the jailhouse window
4. Winnie took Mae's place there
5. How Angus described their situation
6. Everlasting amphibian
7. Month beginning the live-long year
8. Began when Mae got out of window
9. Given in exchange for Winnie's rescue
11. Author
13. Tucks did this to Winnie
14. Giant tree in the center of the wood
15. Jesse's age
17. Mae's philosophy: ___ day at a time
20. Miles removed them from the window
21. What boys did when they got home
22. Angus and Mae made them to sell: wooden ___
24. Mae hit the stranger with this

Tuck Everlasting

STUCK	HORSE	AUGUST	ROWBOAT	SPRING
BUGGY	MILES	WATER	SEVENTEEN	SEVENTY
YEAR	MIDNIGHT	FREE SPACE	WINNIE	IRON
TOAD	TROUT	TOUCH	BARN	WHEEL
CAT	RIFLE	NAILS	TOYS	PEBBLES

Tuck Everlasting

FIREFLIES	CARPENTRY	BABBITT	ASH	DEVIL
LIGHTNING	BLACK	SUIT	POND	WOOD
STRANGER	T	FREE SPACE	RAIN	ONE
TWENTY	SWIM	BLANKET	MUSIC	ANGUS
CEMETERY	EIGHTY	TEN	BLEW	SELL

Tuck Everlasting

BABBITT	BUGGY	MILES	CARPENTRY	ROWBOAT
STRANGER	TROUT	NAILS	SUIT	STUCK
LIGHTNING	TOUCH	FREE SPACE	CONSTABLE	RAIN
HORSE	IRON	EIGHTY	BLACK	ONE
YEAR	TOAD	MAE	TWENTY	WINNIE

Tuck Everlasting

SELL	WOOD	CURSE	AUGUST	ELVES
TREEGAP	TOYS	T	SEVENTEEN	RIFLE
ANGUS	WHEEL	FREE SPACE	ASH	DEVIL
BARN	FIREFLIES	JAIL	BLANKET	PEBBLES
ANNA	SPRING	CAT	SEVENTY	BLEW

Tuck Everlasting

BABBITT	EIGHTY	ANNA	SEVENTY	PEBBLES
TROUT	STUCK	RAIN	TOAD	ONE
DEVIL	JAIL	FREE SPACE	WHEEL	T
BLEW	SWIM	MILES	WINDOW	NAILS
TEN	KIDNAPPED	CONSTABLE	SELL	AUGUST

Tuck Everlasting

BUGGY	YEAR	WOOD	LIGHTNING	ASH
STRANGER	ELVES	MUSIC	ANGUS	ROWBOAT
CEMETERY	BLACK	FREE SPACE	FIREFLIES	JESSE
BARN	WATER	HORSE	BLANKET	TOYS
SPRING	MIDNIGHT	SEVENTEEN	RIFLE	MAE

Tuck Everlasting

PEBBLES	ASH	SEVENTY	DEVIL	ONE
TEN	IRON	ANNA	AUGUST	BARN
JESSE	BLANKET	FREE SPACE	TOUCH	FIREFLIES
NAILS	CAT	TREEGAP	ROWBOAT	ANGUS
WHEEL	EIGHTY	BLACK	HORSE	WINDOW

Tuck Everlasting

MILES	FOSTERS	JAIL	MAE	MUSIC
POND	SELL	RAIN	CEMETERY	ELVES
BLEW	STRANGER	FREE SPACE	TROUT	SEVENTEEN
SUIT	BABBITT	WOOD	KIDNAPPED	YEAR
SWIM	TWENTY	TOAD	CARPENTRY	WINNIE

Tuck Everlasting

ASH	SEVENTEEN	ELVES	TROUT	FOSTERS
SPRING	TEN	TOUCH	EIGHTY	TREEGAP
AUGUST	FIREFLIES	FREE SPACE	STUCK	RAIN
WINDOW	PEBBLES	MIDNIGHT	MUSIC	ONE
ANNA	MAE	KIDNAPPED	IRON	YEAR

Tuck Everlasting

CARPENTRY	TOYS	TWENTY	JESSE	MILES
CEMETERY	BUGGY	ROWBOAT	JAIL	T
SWIM	RIFLE	FREE SPACE	WINNIE	BLANKET
ANGUS	CAT	CONSTABLE	SEVENTY	WHEEL
BLACK	CURSE	BLEW	SUIT	POND

Tuck Everlasting

WOOD	ANNA	SWIM	CURSE	CARPENTRY
MILES	KIDNAPPED	IRON	RIFLE	JESSE
TWENTY	TREEGAP	FREE SPACE	PEBBLES	SELL
TOUCH	TEN	FOSTERS	YEAR	CAT
CONSTABLE	SEVENTY	FIREFLIES	MAE	SEVENTEEN

Tuck Everlasting

HORSE	RAIN	ROWBOAT	ANGUS	BLACK
TOYS	STRANGER	WHEEL	JAIL	BLANKET
WINNIE	STUCK	FREE SPACE	ELVES	TOAD
BABBITT	NAILS	AUGUST	MUSIC	ONE
SPRING	DEVIL	CEMETERY	BLEW	MIDNIGHT

Tuck Everlasting

IRON	HORSE	WHEEL	BARN	MAE
CAT	TROUT	RIFLE	AUGUST	TWENTY
ROWBOAT	ONE	FREE SPACE	EIGHTY	SEVENTY
CEMETERY	SPRING	TOYS	WATER	BLEW
BLANKET	BLACK	ANNA	JESSE	SEVENTEEN

Tuck Everlasting

TOUCH	CURSE	ASH	DEVIL	TREEGAP
TOAD	SUIT	FIREFLIES	CONSTABLE	STRANGER
ANGUS	STUCK	FREE SPACE	PEBBLES	MIDNIGHT
FOSTERS	MUSIC	ELVES	WOOD	WINDOW
TEN	BUGGY	BABBITT	POND	SELL

Tuck Everlasting

SEVENTY	MILES	MIDNIGHT	PEBBLES	CURSE
ROWBOAT	NAILS	WINNIE	HORSE	ASH
RAIN	BARN	FREE SPACE	SWIM	CARPENTRY
DEVIL	WATER	TWENTY	WHEEL	STRANGER
TREEGAP	BLANKET	T	STUCK	SPRING

Tuck Everlasting

CEMETERY	ELVES	RIFLE	IRON	TOYS
TOUCH	LIGHTNING	ANNA	FOSTERS	TOAD
BUGGY	ANGUS	FREE SPACE	TEN	EIGHTY
SEVENTEEN	YEAR	SUIT	MAE	FIREFLIES
CAT	JESSE	BLACK	MUSIC	TROUT

Tuck Everlasting

SPRING	BLANKET	JESSE	MILES	PEBBLES
BLEW	LIGHTNING	MUSIC	SEVENTEEN	BLACK
NAILS	WINNIE	FREE SPACE	IRON	TOUCH
CEMETERY	ONE	YEAR	RAIN	WATER
WHEEL	TROUT	KIDNAPPED	BARN	ROWBOAT

Tuck Everlasting

CONSTABLE	CARPENTRY	BUGGY	FIREFLIES	STRANGER
TWENTY	TEN	DEVIL	HORSE	EIGHTY
ANGUS	MAE	FREE SPACE	TOAD	STUCK
JAIL	SEVENTY	SELL	SWIM	WOOD
POND	RIFLE	FOSTERS	BABBITT	ASH

Tuck Everlasting

FIREFLIES	CAT	STUCK	TWENTY	EIGHTY
BABBITT	WINDOW	MILES	STRANGER	ROWBOAT
IRON	TREEGAP	FREE SPACE	WOOD	YEAR
LIGHTNING	KIDNAPPED	SWIM	WHEEL	SUIT
BLANKET	JAIL	DEVIL	CONSTABLE	ASH

Tuck Everlasting

MAE	BLACK	MUSIC	ANGUS	MIDNIGHT
ELVES	FOSTERS	CEMETERY	TROUT	RIFLE
AUGUST	PEBBLES	FREE SPACE	TOAD	TOYS
CURSE	RAIN	SEVENTEEN	T	NAILS
SELL	TEN	CARPENTRY	WINNIE	SPRING

Tuck Everlasting

RIFLE	WINNIE	WOOD	TROUT	CARPENTRY
YEAR	LIGHTNING	TREEGAP	T	MILES
SWIM	BLEW	FREE SPACE	JESSE	SUIT
ANGUS	ELVES	ROWBOAT	ONE	DEVIL
TWENTY	RAIN	BUGGY	FIREFLIES	WATER

Tuck Everlasting

ANNA	AUGUST	MAE	BLACK	ASH
STUCK	SEVENTEEN	SELL	HORSE	WHEEL
CURSE	FOSTERS	FREE SPACE	CONSTABLE	TOAD
JAIL	KIDNAPPED	SEVENTY	POND	MIDNIGHT
EIGHTY	WINDOW	BABBITT	NAILS	MUSIC

Tuck Everlasting

STRANGER	BLEW	EIGHTY	T	LIGHTNING
YEAR	JESSE	STUCK	TOYS	TOAD
MUSIC	HORSE	FREE SPACE	FOSTERS	BLACK
MIDNIGHT	TREEGAP	SELL	RIFLE	NAILS
WINDOW	TEN	WINNIE	MAE	BABBITT

Tuck Everlasting

TOUCH	SEVENTEEN	BLANKET	POND	SWIM
ASH	BARN	SUIT	JAIL	DEVIL
BUGGY	TWENTY	FREE SPACE	PEBBLES	ANNA
SEVENTY	WATER	MILES	CEMETERY	IRON
CONSTABLE	TROUT	WOOD	CARPENTRY	FIREFLIES

Tuck Everlasting

PEBBLES	SEVENTEEN	SEVENTY	WHEEL	T
TROUT	HORSE	STRANGER	SELL	BUGGY
ANNA	CARPENTRY	FREE SPACE	SWIM	RAIN
LIGHTNING	WATER	BARN	TEN	BABBITT
JESSE	MIDNIGHT	TWENTY	DEVIL	WINNIE

Tuck Everlasting

MAE	CURSE	POND	BLANKET	SUIT
CAT	ONE	EIGHTY	ASH	MUSIC
TOUCH	YEAR	FREE SPACE	BLACK	FOSTERS
TOYS	STUCK	CONSTABLE	BLEW	IRON
TREEGAP	ANGUS	TOAD	KIDNAPPED	NAILS

Tuck Everlasting

JAIL	PEBBLES	SELL	STUCK	STRANGER
TOYS	LIGHTNING	NAILS	BLEW	SEVENTY
RIFLE	ANNA	FREE SPACE	EIGHTY	BUGGY
WHEEL	FIREFLIES	DEVIL	SPRING	BLANKET
CONSTABLE	MAE	CURSE	CARPENTRY	TROUT

Tuck Everlasting

AUGUST	FOSTERS	MUSIC	WINDOW	IRON
CAT	ANGUS	CEMETERY	SUIT	HORSE
MIDNIGHT	ASH	FREE SPACE	BLACK	TWENTY
TREEGAP	T	JESSE	ONE	RAIN
YEAR	TOAD	WATER	POND	MILES

Tuck Everlasting

ANGUS	ELVES	IRON	BLACK	JESSE
JAIL	STRANGER	TOUCH	SELL	PEBBLES
FIREFLIES	BARN	FREE SPACE	KIDNAPPED	T
TWENTY	SEVENTEEN	ROWBOAT	BLEW	CARPENTRY
CURSE	RAIN	BABBITT	WOOD	WHEEL

Tuck Everlasting

TOAD	YEAR	RIFLE	HORSE	BLANKET
POND	BUGGY	WATER	CAT	DEVIL
NAILS	MUSIC	FREE SPACE	TROUT	STUCK
SWIM	AUGUST	FOSTERS	MILES	TREEGAP
TOYS	WINNIE	WINDOW	EIGHTY	SEVENTY

Tuck Everlasting

NAILS	FOSTERS	TOUCH	CURSE	SWIM
ANNA	YEAR	PEBBLES	BARN	WHEEL
BLEW	POND	FREE SPACE	HORSE	RIFLE
WATER	KIDNAPPED	ELVES	BABBITT	CEMETERY
SELL	TEN	CAT	BLACK	WINDOW

Tuck Everlasting

EIGHTY	STUCK	LIGHTNING	WINNIE	JESSE
SPRING	ROWBOAT	JAIL	MAE	TWENTY
RAIN	SEVENTY	FREE SPACE	MILES	BUGGY
MIDNIGHT	DEVIL	CARPENTRY	STRANGER	CONSTABLE
SUIT	SEVENTEEN	TOAD	ANGUS	TROUT

Tuck Everlasting Vocabulary Word List

No.	Word	Clue/Definition
1.	ACCOMMODATIONS	lodging
2.	ACCOMPLICE	partner; accessory
3.	ACRID	bitter; harsh
4.	ANGUISH	pain; suffering
5.	APPEALING	pleasing; charming
6.	ASSURANCE	confidence: self-___
7.	BARBARIAN	savage; brute
8.	BOVINE	sleepy; cow-like
9.	CAHOOTS	partnership
10.	CAVERNOUS	hollow and deep sounding
11.	CONSOLINGLY	comfortingly; soothingly
12.	DECISIVELY	with determination
13.	DEPRECATION	disapproval of self; self-___
14.	DISTRACTEDLY	in bewilderment; confusedly
15.	ELATED	thrilled ; overjoyed
16.	ENVIOUS	jealous; resentful
17.	EXTRAORDINARY	amazing; remarkable
18.	EXULTANT	ecstatic; thrilled
19.	FLAILING	thrashing
20.	FORLORN	miserable; forsaken
21.	GALLING	annoying; irritating
22.	GALLOWS	hanging structure
23.	GANDER	look
24.	GENTILITY	elegance; grace
25.	GHASTLY	dreadful; horrible
26.	ILLITERATES	unlearned; ignorant people
27.	IMMENSE	giant; huge
28.	INDOMITABLE	supreme; unconquerable
29.	INFINITE	limitless
30.	IRRELEVANTLY	in a 'beside the point' manner
31.	LUXURIOUS	elegant; rich
32.	MARIONETTE	puppet
33.	MEAGER	skimpy; sparse
34.	MELANCHOLY	gloomy; woeful
35.	METAPHYSICS	branch of science
36.	OPPRESSIVE	heavy; stifling
37.	ORDEAL	burden; trial
38.	PARSON	minister; preacher
39.	PERIL	danger
40.	PERILOUS	dangerous
41.	PERVERSELY	uncontrollably
42.	PETULANCE	crossness; irritability
43.	PLAINTIVELY	sorrowfully
44.	PONDEROUS	dull; dreary
45.	PROSTRATE	worn out; exhausted
46.	RECEDED	lessened; subsided
47.	REMORSELESS	without regret
48.	REVOLUTIONARY	rebellious; unique
49.	REVULSION	disgust; distaste
50.	ROUST	to bring out of a state of sleep
51.	RUEFUL	mournful; pitiful

Tuck Everlasting Vocabulary Word List Continued

No.	Word	Clue/Definition
52.	SEDATELY	calmly
53.	SKELTER	every which way; no pattern: helter-___
54.	STAUNCHLY	loyally; faithfully
55.	SUBMISSION	obedience; meekness
56.	TANGENT	departure
57.	TEEMING	bustling; swarming
58.	TRANQUIL	calm; peaceful
59.	UNFLINCHINGLY	unafraid; not hesitant

Tuck Everlasting Vocabulary Fill In The Blanks 1

_____ 1. rebellious; unique

_____ 2. hollow and deep sounding

_____ 3. burden; trial

_____ 4. amazing; remarkable

_____ 5. thrilled ; overjoyed

_____ 6. partner; accessory

_____ 7. jealous; resentful

_____ 8. bustling; swarming

_____ 9. limitless

_____ 10. dreadful; horrible

_____ 11. miserable; forsaken

_____ 12. pain; suffering

_____ 13. departure

_____ 14. danger

_____ 15. without regret

_____ 16. unafraid; not hesitant

_____ 17. loyally; faithfully

_____ 18. bitter; harsh

_____ 19. giant; huge

_____ 20. comfortingly; soothingly

Tuck Everlasting Vocabulary Fill In The Blanks 1 Answer Key

REVOLUTIONARY	1. rebellious; unique
CAVERNOUS	2. hollow and deep sounding
ORDEAL	3. burden; trial
EXTRAORDINARY	4. amazing; remarkable
ELATED	5. thrilled; overjoyed
ACCOMPLICE	6. partner; accessory
ENVIOUS	7. jealous; resentful
TEEMING	8. bustling; swarming
INFINITE	9. limitless
GHASTLY	10. dreadful; horrible
FORLORN	11. miserable; forsaken
ANGUISH	12. pain; suffering
TANGENT	13. departure
PERIL	14. danger
REMORSELESS	15. without regret
UNFLINCHINGLY	16. unafraid; not hesitant
STAUNCHLY	17. loyally; faithfully
ACRID	18. bitter; harsh
IMMENSE	19. giant; huge
CONSOLINGLY	20. comfortingly; soothingly

Tuck Everlasting Vocabulary Fill In The Blanks 2

_____ 1. sorrowfully
_____ 2. dreadful; horrible
_____ 3. uncontrollably
_____ 4. confidence: self-___
_____ 5. heavy; stifling
_____ 6. calmly
_____ 7. elegant; rich
_____ 8. bustling; swarming
_____ 9. puppet
_____ 10. unlearned; ignorant people
_____ 11. look
_____ 12. crossness; irritability
_____ 13. loyally; faithfully
_____ 14. obedience; meekness
_____ 15. unafraid; not hesitant
_____ 16. disgust; distaste
_____ 17. calm; peaceful
_____ 18. departure
_____ 19. miserable; forsaken
_____ 20. branch of science

Tuck Everlasting Vocabulary Fill In The Blanks 2 Answer Key

PLAINTIVELY	1. sorrowfully
GHASTLY	2. dreadful; horrible
PERVERSELY	3. uncontrollably
ASSURANCE	4. confidence: self-___
OPPRESSIVE	5. heavy; stifling
SEDATELY	6. calmly
LUXURIOUS	7. elegant; rich
TEEMING	8. bustling; swarming
MARIONETTE	9. puppet
ILLITERATES	10. unlearned; ignorant people
GANDER	11. look
PETULANCE	12. crossness; irritability
STAUNCHLY	13. loyally; faithfully
SUBMISSION	14. obedience; meekness
UNFLINCHINGLY	15. unafraid; not hesitant
REVULSION	16. disgust; distaste
TRANQUIL	17. calm; peaceful
TANGENT	18. departure
FORLORN	19. miserable; forsaken
METAPHYSICS	20. branch of science

Tuck Everlasting Vocabulary Fill In The Blanks 3

_____ 1. skimpy; sparse
_____ 2. without regret
_____ 3. calmly
_____ 4. calm; peaceful
_____ 5. confidence: self-___
_____ 6. partner; accessory
_____ 7. comfortingly; soothingly
_____ 8. dreadful; horrible
_____ 9. uncontrollably
_____ 10. danger
_____ 11. hollow and deep sounding
_____ 12. miserable; forsaken
_____ 13. unlearned; ignorant people
_____ 14. unafraid; not hesitant
_____ 15. savage; brute
_____ 16. pain; suffering
_____ 17. jealous; resentful
_____ 18. dangerous
_____ 19. hanging structure
_____ 20. sleepy; cow-like

Tuck Everlasting Vocabulary Fill In The Blanks 3 Answer Key

MEAGER	1. skimpy; sparse
REMORSELESS	2. without regret
SEDATELY	3. calmly
TRANQUIL	4. calm; peaceful
ASSURANCE	5. confidence: self-___
ACCOMPLICE	6. partner; accessory
CONSOLINGLY	7. comfortingly; soothingly
GHASTLY	8. dreadful; horrible
PERVERSELY	9. uncontrollably
PERIL	10. danger
CAVERNOUS	11. hollow and deep sounding
FORLORN	12. miserable; forsaken
ILLITERATES	13. unlearned; ignorant people
UNFLINCHINGLY	14. unafraid; not hesitant
BARBARIAN	15. savage; brute
ANGUISH	16. pain; suffering
ENVIOUS	17. jealous; resentful
PERILOUS	18. dangerous
GALLOWS	19. hanging structure
BOVINE	20. sleepy; cow-like

Tuck Everlasting Vocabulary Fill In The Blanks 4

_____ 1. giant; huge

_____ 2. dangerous

_____ 3. look

_____ 4. savage; brute

_____ 5. elegance; grace

_____ 6. in bewilderment; confusedly

_____ 7. heavy; stifling

_____ 8. with determination

_____ 9. burden; trial

_____ 10. mournful; pitiful

_____ 11. pain; suffering

_____ 12. uncontrollably

_____ 13. partnership

_____ 14. supreme; unconquerable

_____ 15. loyally; faithfully

_____ 16. hanging structure

_____ 17. thrilled ; overjoyed

_____ 18. calmly

_____ 19. jealous; resentful

_____ 20. in a 'beside the point' manner

Tuck Everlasting Vocabulary Fill In The Blanks 4 Answer Key

IMMENSE	1. giant; huge
PERILOUS	2. dangerous
GANDER	3. look
BARBARIAN	4. savage; brute
GENTILITY	5. elegance; grace
DISTRACTEDLY	6. in bewilderment; confusedly
OPPRESSIVE	7. heavy; stifling
DECISIVELY	8. with determination
ORDEAL	9. burden; trial
RUEFUL	10. mournful; pitiful
ANGUISH	11. pain; suffering
PERVERSELY	12. uncontrollably
CAHOOTS	13. partnership
INDOMITABLE	14. supreme; unconquerable
STAUNCHLY	15. loyally; faithfully
GALLOWS	16. hanging structure
ELATED	17. thrilled; overjoyed
SEDATELY	18. calmly
ENVIOUS	19. jealous; resentful
IRRELEVANTLY	20. in a 'beside the point' manner

Tuck Everlasting Vocabulary Matching 1

___ 1. FLAILING   A. partner; accessory
___ 2. IRRELEVANTLY   B. to bring out of a state of sleep
___ 3. REVOLUTIONARY   C. disapproval of self; self-___
___ 4. ROUST   D. in a 'beside the point' manner
___ 5. ACCOMPLICE   E. hollow and deep sounding
___ 6. CAVERNOUS   F. rebellious; unique
___ 7. LUXURIOUS   G. worn out; exhausted
___ 8. DEPRECATION   H. crossness; irritability
___ 9. PETULANCE   I. obedience; meekness
___10. BOVINE   J. puppet
___11. ACRID   K. bitter; harsh
___12. RECEDED   L. dull; dreary
___13. ILLITERATES   M. sleepy; cow-like
___14. MARIONETTE   N. supreme; unconquerable
___15. REVULSION   O. annoying; irritating
___16. SUBMISSION   P. pleasing; charming
___17. EXTRAORDINARY   Q. lessened; subsided
___18. PROSTRATE   R. every which way; no pattern: helter-___
___19. ACCOMMODATIONS   S. amazing; remarkable
___20. SKELTER   T. disgust; distaste
___21. INDOMITABLE   U. elegant; rich
___22. PONDEROUS   V. thrashing
___23. TEEMING   W. unlearned; ignorant people
___24. APPEALING   X. lodging
___25. GALLING   Y. bustling; swarming

Tuck Everlasting Vocabulary Matching 1 Answer Key

V - 1.	FLAILING	A. partner; accessory
D - 2.	IRRELEVANTLY	B. to bring out of a state of sleep
F - 3.	REVOLUTIONARY	C. disapproval of self; self-___
B - 4.	ROUST	D. in a 'beside the point' manner
A - 5.	ACCOMPLICE	E. hollow and deep sounding
E - 6.	CAVERNOUS	F. rebellious; unique
U - 7.	LUXURIOUS	G. worn out; exhausted
C - 8.	DEPRECATION	H. crossness; irritability
H - 9.	PETULANCE	I. obedience; meekness
M -10.	BOVINE	J. puppet
K -11.	ACRID	K. bitter; harsh
Q -12.	RECEDED	L. dull; dreary
W -13.	ILLITERATES	M. sleepy; cow-like
J -14.	MARIONETTE	N. supreme; unconquerable
T -15.	REVULSION	O. annoying; irritating
I -16.	SUBMISSION	P. pleasing; charming
S -17.	EXTRAORDINARY	Q. lessened; subsided
G -18.	PROSTRATE	R. every which way; no pattern: helter-___
X -19.	ACCOMMODATIONS	S. amazing; remarkable
R -20.	SKELTER	T. disgust; distaste
N -21.	INDOMITABLE	U. elegant; rich
L -22.	PONDEROUS	V. thrashing
Y -23.	TEEMING	W. unlearned; ignorant people
P -24.	APPEALING	X. lodging
O -25.	GALLING	Y. bustling; swarming

Tuck Everlasting Vocabulary Matching 2

___ 1. ENVIOUS   A. jealous; resentful
___ 2. PERILOUS   B. dangerous
___ 3. INDOMITABLE   C. disapproval of self; self-___
___ 4. PLAINTIVELY   D. look
___ 5. TANGENT   E. thrashing
___ 6. IMMENSE   F. without regret
___ 7. SKELTER   G. calm; peaceful
___ 8. GHASTLY   H. unafraid; not hesitant
___ 9. BARBARIAN   I. thrilled ; overjoyed
___10. REMORSELESS   J. giant; huge
___11. LUXURIOUS   K. dreadful; horrible
___12. TRANQUIL   L. ecstatic; thrilled
___13. FLAILING   M. with determination
___14. ROUST   N. mournful; pitiful
___15. UNFLINCHINGLY   O. loyally; faithfully
___16. ELATED   P. every which way; no pattern: helter-___
___17. GANDER   Q. to bring out of a state of sleep
___18. PERIL   R. danger
___19. RUEFUL   S. supreme; unconquerable
___20. STAUNCHLY   T. departure
___21. ORDEAL   U. savage; brute
___22. DEPRECATION   V. crossness; irritability
___23. DECISIVELY   W. sorrowfully
___24. EXULTANT   X. burden; trial
___25. PETULANCE   Y. elegant; rich

Tuck Everlasting Vocabulary Matching 2 Answer Key

A - 1. ENVIOUS	A.	jealous; resentful
B - 2. PERILOUS	B.	dangerous
S - 3. INDOMITABLE	C.	disapproval of self; self-___
W - 4. PLAINTIVELY	D.	look
T - 5. TANGENT	E.	thrashing
J - 6. IMMENSE	F.	without regret
P - 7. SKELTER	G.	calm; peaceful
K - 8. GHASTLY	H.	unafraid; not hesitant
U - 9. BARBARIAN	I.	thrilled; overjoyed
F - 10. REMORSELESS	J.	giant; huge
Y - 11. LUXURIOUS	K.	dreadful; horrible
G - 12. TRANQUIL	L.	ecstatic; thrilled
E - 13. FLAILING	M.	with determination
Q - 14. ROUST	N.	mournful; pitiful
H - 15. UNFLINCHINGLY	O.	loyally; faithfully
I - 16. ELATED	P.	every which way; no pattern: helter-___
D - 17. GANDER	Q.	to bring out of a state of sleep
R - 18. PERIL	R.	danger
N - 19. RUEFUL	S.	supreme; unconquerable
O - 20. STAUNCHLY	T.	departure
X - 21. ORDEAL	U.	savage; brute
C - 22. DEPRECATION	V.	crossness; irritability
M - 23. DECISIVELY	W.	sorrowfully
L - 24. EXULTANT	X.	burden; trial
V - 25. PETULANCE	Y.	elegant; rich

Tuck Everlasting Vocabulary Matching 3

___ 1. RUEFUL   A. hanging structure
___ 2. INFINITE   B. rebellious; unique
___ 3. ASSURANCE   C. puppet
___ 4. FLAILING   D. look
___ 5. TRANQUIL   E. giant; huge
___ 6. TEEMING   F. calmly
___ 7. MELANCHOLY   G. gloomy; woeful
___ 8. ILLITERATES   H. thrashing
___ 9. INDOMITABLE   I. partnership
___10. SEDATELY   J. without regret
___11. ELATED   K. limitless
___12. APPEALING   L. ecstatic; thrilled
___13. MARIONETTE   M. pleasing; charming
___14. DECISIVELY   N. thrilled ; overjoyed
___15. ORDEAL   O. calm; peaceful
___16. CAVERNOUS   P. unafraid; not hesitant
___17. IMMENSE   Q. with determination
___18. METAPHYSICS   R. bustling; swarming
___19. EXULTANT   S. supreme; unconquerable
___20. CAHOOTS   T. hollow and deep sounding
___21. GALLOWS   U. confidence: self-___
___22. REMORSELESS   V. unlearned; ignorant people
___23. UNFLINCHINGLY   W. branch of science
___24. GANDER   X. mournful; pitiful
___25. REVOLUTIONARY   Y. burden; trial

Tuck Everlasting Vocabulary Matching 3 Answer Key

X - 1. RUEFUL	A. hanging structure
K - 2. INFINITE	B. rebellious; unique
U - 3. ASSURANCE	C. puppet
H - 4. FLAILING	D. look
O - 5. TRANQUIL	E. giant; huge
R - 6. TEEMING	F. calmly
G - 7. MELANCHOLY	G. gloomy; woeful
V - 8. ILLITERATES	H. thrashing
S - 9. INDOMITABLE	I. partnership
F - 10. SEDATELY	J. without regret
N - 11. ELATED	K. limitless
M - 12. APPEALING	L. ecstatic; thrilled
C - 13. MARIONETTE	M. pleasing; charming
Q - 14. DECISIVELY	N. thrilled; overjoyed
Y - 15. ORDEAL	O. calm; peaceful
T - 16. CAVERNOUS	P. unafraid; not hesitant
E - 17. IMMENSE	Q. with determination
W - 18. METAPHYSICS	R. bustling; swarming
L - 19. EXULTANT	S. supreme; unconquerable
I - 20. CAHOOTS	T. hollow and deep sounding
A - 21. GALLOWS	U. confidence: self-___
J - 22. REMORSELESS	V. unlearned; ignorant people
P - 23. UNFLINCHINGLY	W. branch of science
D - 24. GANDER	X. mournful; pitiful
B - 25. REVOLUTIONARY	Y. burden; trial

Tuck Everlasting Vocabulary Matching 4

___ 1. CONSOLINGLY   A. sorrowfully
___ 2. FORLORN   B. giant; huge
___ 3. IMMENSE   C. comfortingly; soothingly
___ 4. PERIL   D. calmly
___ 5. EXULTANT   E. lessened; subsided
___ 6. ORDEAL   F. to bring out of a state of sleep
___ 7. ELATED   G. look
___ 8. STAUNCHLY   H. thrilled ; overjoyed
___ 9. ACCOMPLICE   I. worn out; exhausted
___10. GANDER   J. ecstatic; thrilled
___11. GALLOWS   K. loyally; faithfully
___12. SEDATELY   L. pain; suffering
___13. FLAILING   M. partner; accessory
___14. ROUST   N. amazing; remarkable
___15. PROSTRATE   O. mournful; pitiful
___16. MARIONETTE   P. miserable; forsaken
___17. SKELTER   Q. calm; peaceful
___18. EXTRAORDINARY   R. thrashing
___19. ANGUISH   S. puppet
___20. REMORSELESS   T. burden; trial
___21. ENVIOUS   U. hanging structure
___22. PLAINTIVELY   V. danger
___23. RUEFUL   W. every which way; no pattern: helter-___
___24. TRANQUIL   X. without regret
___25. RECEDED   Y. jealous; resentful

Tuck Everlasting Vocabulary Matching 4 Answer Key

C - 1. CONSOLINGLY	A.	sorrowfully
P - 2. FORLORN	B.	giant; huge
B - 3. IMMENSE	C.	comfortingly; soothingly
V - 4. PERIL	D.	calmly
J - 5. EXULTANT	E.	lessened; subsided
T - 6. ORDEAL	F.	to bring out of a state of sleep
H - 7. ELATED	G.	look
K - 8. STAUNCHLY	H.	thrilled ; overjoyed
M - 9. ACCOMPLICE	I.	worn out; exhausted
G -10. GANDER	J.	ecstatic; thrilled
U -11. GALLOWS	K.	loyally; faithfully
D -12. SEDATELY	L.	pain; suffering
R -13. FLAILING	M.	partner; accessory
F -14. ROUST	N.	amazing; remarkable
I -15. PROSTRATE	O.	mournful; pitiful
S -16. MARIONETTE	P.	miserable; forsaken
W -17. SKELTER	Q.	calm; peaceful
N -18. EXTRAORDINARY	R.	thrashing
L -19. ANGUISH	S.	puppet
X -20. REMORSELESS	T.	burden; trial
Y -21. ENVIOUS	U.	hanging structure
A -22. PLAINTIVELY	V.	danger
O -23. RUEFUL	W.	every which way; no pattern: helter-___
Q -24. TRANQUIL	X.	without regret
E -25. RECEDED	Y.	jealous; resentful

Tuck Everlasting Vocabulary Magic Squares 1

Match the definition with the vocabulary word. Put your answers in the magic squares below. When your answers are correct, all columns and rows will add to the same number.

A. IMMENSE
B. ACCOMPLICE
C. RUEFUL
D. ANGUISH
E. INDOMITABLE
F. MELANCHOLY
G. PERVERSELY
H. PONDEROUS
I. PERILOUS
J. ACRID
K. ROUST
L. EXULTANT
M. EXTRAORDINARY
N. UNFLINCHINGLY
O. PETULANCE
P. METAPHYSICS

1. gloomy; woeful
2. dangerous
3. crossness; irritability
4. pain; suffering
5. amazing; remarkable
6. partner; accessory
7. dull; dreary
8. to bring out of a state of sleep
9. mournful; pitiful
10. branch of science
11. bitter; harsh
12. supreme; unconquerable
13. ecstatic; thrilled
14. uncontrollably
15. giant; huge
16. unafraid; not hesitant

A=	B=	C=	D=
E=	F=	G=	H=
I=	J=	K=	L=
M=	N=	O=	P=

Tuck Everlasting Vocabulary Magic Squares 1 Answer Key

Match the definition with the vocabulary word. Put your answers in the magic squares below. When your answers are correct, all columns and rows will add to the same number.

A. IMMENSE
B. ACCOMPLICE
C. RUEFUL
D. ANGUISH
E. INDOMITABLE
F. MELANCHOLY
G. PERVERSELY
H. PONDEROUS
I. PERILOUS
J. ACRID
K. ROUST
L. EXULTANT
M. EXTRAORDINARY
N. UNFLINCHINGLY
O. PETULANCE
P. METAPHYSICS

1. gloomy; woeful
2. dangerous
3. crossness; irritability
4. pain; suffering
5. amazing; remarkable
6. partner; accessory
7. dull; dreary
8. to bring out of a state of sleep
9. mournful; pitiful
10. branch of science
11. bitter; harsh
12. supreme; unconquerable
13. ecstatic; thrilled
14. uncontrollably
15. giant; huge
16. unafraid; not hesitant

A=15	B=6	C=9	D=4
E=12	F=1	G=14	H=7
I=2	J=11	K=8	L=13
M=5	N=16	O=3	P=10

Tuck Everlasting Vocabulary Magic Squares 2

Match the definition with the vocabulary word. Put your answers in the magic squares below. When your answers are correct, all columns and rows will add to the same number.

A. INDOMITABLE
B. ELATED
C. ENVIOUS
D. INFINITE
E. FORLORN
F. SEDATELY
G. TANGENT
H. APPEALING
I. PLAINTIVELY
J. IRRELEVANTLY
K. REVULSION
L. LUXURIOUS
M. CONSOLINGLY
N. RECEDED
O. SUBMISSION
P. ORDEAL

1. obedience; meekness
2. limitless
3. in a 'beside the point' manner
4. miserable; forsaken
5. sorrowfully
6. calmly
7. burden; trial
8. jealous; resentful
9. pleasing; charming
10. disgust; distaste
11. supreme; unconquerable
12. lessened; subsided
13. thrilled; overjoyed
14. comfortingly; soothingly
15. departure
16. elegant; rich

A=	B=	C=	D=
E=	F=	G=	H=
I=	J=	K=	L=
M=	N=	O=	P=

Tuck Everlasting Vocabulary Magic Squares 2 Answer Key

Match the definition with the vocabulary word. Put your answers in the magic squares below. When your answers are correct, all columns and rows will add to the same number.

A. INDOMITABLE
B. ELATED
C. ENVIOUS
D. INFINITE
E. FORLORN
F. SEDATELY
G. TANGENT
H. APPEALING
I. PLAINTIVELY
J. IRRELEVANTLY
K. REVULSION
L. LUXURIOUS
M. CONSOLINGLY
N. RECEDED
O. SUBMISSION
P. ORDEAL

1. obedience; meekness
2. limitless
3. in a 'beside the point' manner
4. miserable; forsaken
5. sorrowfully
6. calmly
7. burden; trial
8. jealous; resentful
9. pleasing; charming
10. disgust; distaste
11. supreme; unconquerable
12. lessened; subsided
13. thrilled; overjoyed
14. comfortingly; soothingly
15. departure
16. elegant; rich

A=11	B=13	C=8	D=2
E=4	F=6	G=15	H=9
I=5	J=3	K=10	L=16
M=14	N=12	O=1	P=7

Tuck Everlasting Vocabulary Magic Squares 3

Match the definition with the vocabulary word. Put your answers in the magic squares below. When your answers are correct, all columns and rows will add to the same number.

A. PERVERSELY
B. ENVIOUS
C. DISTRACTEDLY
D. RUEFUL
E. ACCOMPLICE
F. MELANCHOLY
G. ROUST
H. PARSON
I. MARIONETTE
J. METAPHYSICS
K. GALLING
L. CAVERNOUS
M. DECISIVELY
N. EXULTANT
O. BOVINE
P. PERIL

1. with determination
2. gloomy; woeful
3. minister; preacher
4. sleepy; cow-like
5. hollow and deep sounding
6. in bewilderment; confusedly
7. uncontrollably
8. branch of science
9. annoying; irritating
10. mournful; pitiful
11. jealous; resentful
12. puppet
13. ecstatic; thrilled
14. partner; accessory
15. to bring out of a state of sleep
16. danger

A=	B=	C=	D=
E=	F=	G=	H=
I=	J=	K=	L=
M=	N=	O=	P=

Tuck Everlasting Vocabulary Magic Squares 3 Answer Key

Match the definition with the vocabulary word. Put your answers in the magic squares below. When your answers are correct, all columns and rows will add to the same number.

A. PERVERSELY
B. ENVIOUS
C. DISTRACTEDLY
D. RUEFUL
E. ACCOMPLICE
F. MELANCHOLY
G. ROUST
H. PARSON
I. MARIONETTE
J. METAPHYSICS
K. GALLING
L. CAVERNOUS
M. DECISIVELY
N. EXULTANT
O. BOVINE
P. PERIL

1. with determination
2. gloomy; woeful
3. minister; preacher
4. sleepy; cow-like
5. hollow and deep sounding
6. in bewilderment; confusedly
7. uncontrollably
8. branch of science
9. annoying; irritating
10. mournful; pitiful
11. jealous; resentful
12. puppet
13. ecstatic; thrilled
14. partner; accessory
15. to bring out of a state of sleep
16. danger

A=7	B=11	C=6	D=10
E=14	F=2	G=15	H=3
I=12	J=8	K=9	L=5
M=1	N=13	O=4	P=16

Tuck Everlasting Vocabulary Magic Squares 4

Match the definition with the vocabulary word. Put your answers in the magic squares below. When your answers are correct, all columns and rows will add to the same number.

A. APPEALING
B. REVOLUTIONARY
C. FLAILING
D. PROSTRATE
E. ELATED
F. ACCOMPLICE
G. BARBARIAN
H. IRRELEVANTLY
I. REMORSELESS
J. REVULSION
K. STAUNCHLY
L. PERVERSELY
M. ASSURANCE
N. PONDEROUS
O. EXTRAORDINARY
P. IMMENSE

1. pleasing; charming
2. dull; dreary
3. disgust; distaste
4. thrilled ; overjoyed
5. savage; brute
6. uncontrollably
7. giant; huge
8. thrashing
9. amazing; remarkable
10. worn out; exhausted
11. in a 'beside the point' manner
12. loyally; faithfully
13. without regret
14. partner; accessory
15. rebellious; unique
16. confidence: self-___

A=	B=	C=	D=
E=	F=	G=	H=
I=	J=	K=	L=
M=	N=	O=	P=

Tuck Everlasting Vocabulary Magic Squares 4 Answer Key

Match the definition with the vocabulary word. Put your answers in the magic squares below. When your answers are correct, all columns and rows will add to the same number.

A. APPEALING
B. REVOLUTIONARY
C. FLAILING
D. PROSTRATE
E. ELATED
F. ACCOMPLICE
G. BARBARIAN
H. IRRELEVANTLY
I. REMORSELESS
J. REVULSION
K. STAUNCHLY
L. PERVERSELY
M. ASSURANCE
N. PONDEROUS
O. EXTRAORDINARY
P. IMMENSE

1. pleasing; charming
2. dull; dreary
3. disgust; distaste
4. thrilled ; overjoyed
5. savage; brute
6. uncontrollably
7. giant; huge
8. thrashing
9. amazing; remarkable
10. worn out; exhausted
11. in a 'beside the point' manner
12. loyally; faithfully
13. without regret
14. partner; accessory
15. rebellious; unique
16. confidence: self-___

A=1	B=15	C=8	D=10
E=4	F=14	G=5	H=11
I=13	J=3	K=12	L=6
M=16	N=2	O=9	P=7

Tuck Everlasting Vocabulary Word Search 1

Words are placed backwards, forward, diagonally, up and down. Clues listed below can help you find the words. Circle the hidden vocabulary words in the maze.

```
D I S T R A C T E D L Y F L A I L I N G
C Z T A N G U I S H A L O I T M K R A F
C A V E R N O U S B S E R U D E M E I K
I R E C E D E D J G S V L Q E A S V R S
D N K Z Y M K R N F U I O N X G L U A G
G Q F N C M I I M P R T A T E E L B C
I S V I F O L N E Z A N N R R L S R S
R W M Z N A N R G R N I F T A L B I A H
R O F F E I I S R Q C A F W O U A O B D
E L N P B L T V O U E L P R R X T N B G
L L P M O N H E N L E P T C D U I M E H
E A T U R E D N A G I F R S I R M E T X
V G S R D J L R R E Z N U D N I O L A W
A Z A R E R E A C T C O G L A O D A R B
N R L L A T S W T T R N N L R U N T N
T N A T L U X E M E T A P H Y S I C S P
L Z D E O I S Y D N D E R N N E A H O L
Y T K I D N N N E O R X Z Z N H R O R Z
Z S V Z E N O G D I R C A I O O G L P V
M N K M C P N V L R X Q V O U Q N Y B S
E Z M H H A N W S A C O T S P A R S O N
H I Y L T S A H G M B S T A U N C H L Y
```

amazing; remarkable (13)
annoying; irritating (7)
bitter; harsh (5)
branch of science (11)
burden; trial (6)
bustling; swarming (7)
calm; peaceful (8)
comfortingly; soothingly (11)
confidence: self-___ (9)
danger (5)
dangerous (8)
departure (7)
disgust; distaste (9)
dreadful; horrible (7)
dull; dreary (9)
ecstatic; thrilled (8)
elegant; rich (9)
every which way; no pattern: helter-___ (7)
giant; huge (7)
gloomy; woeful (10)
hanging structure (7)
hollow and deep sounding (9)
in a 'beside the point' manner (12)

in bewilderment; confusedly (12)
jealous; resentful (7)
lessened; subsided (7)
limitless (8)
look (6)
loyally; faithfully (9)
minister; preacher (6)
miserable; forsaken (7)
mournful; pitiful (6)
pain; suffering (7)
partnership (7)
pleasing; charming (9)
puppet (10)
savage; brute (9)
skimpy; sparse (6)
sleepy; cow-like (6)
sorrowfully (11)
supreme; unconquerable (11)
thrashing (8)
thrilled; overjoyed (6)
to bring out of a state of sleep (5)
worn out; exhausted (9)

Tuck Everlasting Vocabulary Word Search 1 Answer Key

Words are placed backwards, forward, diagonally, up and down. Clues listed below can help you find the words. Circle the hidden vocabulary words in the maze.

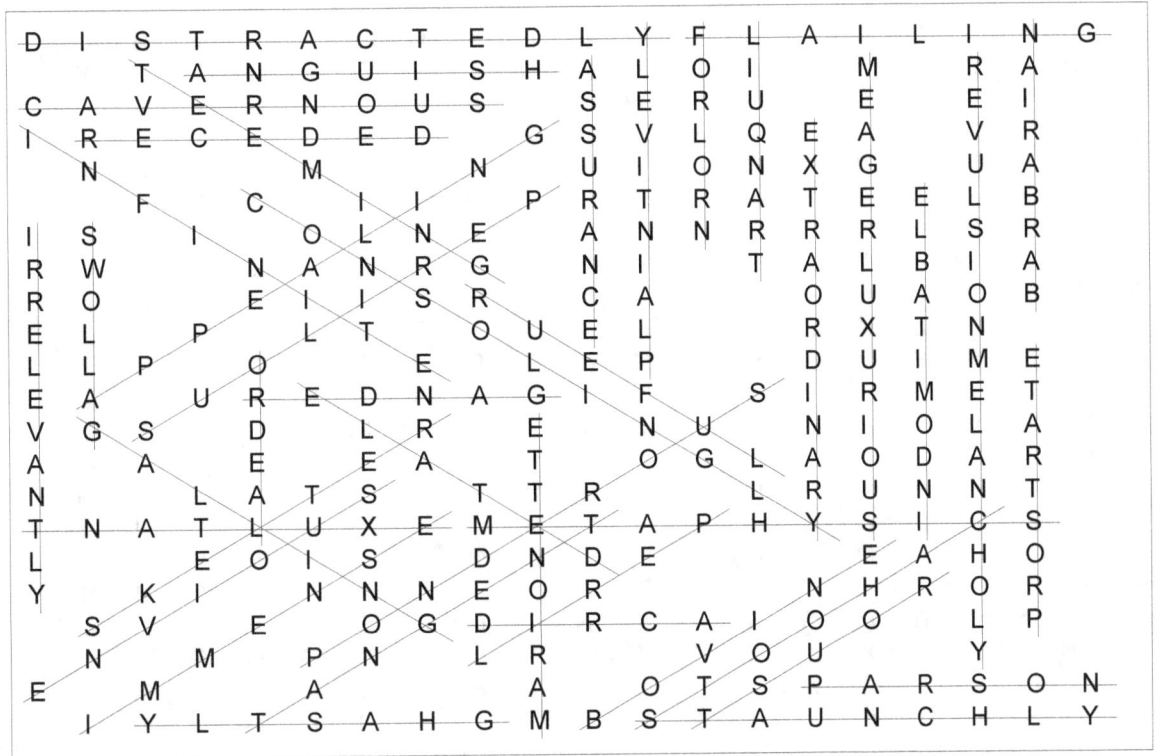

amazing; remarkable (13)
annoying; irritating (7)
bitter; harsh (5)
branch of science (11)
burden; trial (6)
bustling; swarming (7)
calm; peaceful (8)
comfortingly; soothingly (11)
confidence: self-___ (9)
danger (5)
dangerous (8)
departure (7)
disgust; distaste (9)
dreadful; horrible (7)
dull; dreary (9)
ecstatic; thrilled (8)
elegant; rich (9)
every which way; no pattern: helter-___ (7)
giant; huge (7)
gloomy; woeful (10)
hanging structure (7)
hollow and deep sounding (9)
in a 'beside the point' manner (12)

in bewilderment; confusedly (12)
jealous; resentful (7)
lessened; subsided (7)
limitless (8)
look (6)
loyally; faithfully (9)
minister; preacher (6)
miserable; forsaken (7)
mournful; pitiful (6)
pain; suffering (7)
partnership (7)
pleasing; charming (9)
puppet (10)
savage; brute (9)
skimpy; sparse (6)
sleepy; cow-like (6)
sorrowfully (11)
supreme; unconquerable (11)
thrashing (8)
thrilled; overjoyed (6)
to bring out of a state of sleep (5)
worn out; exhausted (9)

Tuck Everlasting Vocabulary Word Search 2

Words are placed backwards, forward, diagonally, up and down. Clues listed below can help you find the words. Circle the hidden vocabulary words in the maze.

```
S F V O P A C C O M P L I C E S S R B G
K O R P E S V G R X K D J L S E T U O M
E R T P T S X A D W M H A E D T O E V C
L L T R U U N L E B G T L A E A O F I W
T O E E L R O L A T E E T G X R H U N Y
E R E S A A I I L D S E N B U E A L E S
R N M S N N T N N R L I W Y L T C V T P
L M I I C C A G O Y L R B C T I G G A B
D P N V E E C M G A N D E R A L A J N L
L E G E Z K E J E D C V N F N L L D G J
U R F S P R R P Q G D Z F B T I L Y E J
X V E C C F P H S I U G N A Y N O T N V
U E R V W A E C P T M D Q L X F W P T B
R R E Z U G D G E A Y M G F S I S E R G
I S C T F L G H N X R N E W G N G R A G
O E E F I Q S C V F I S Q N J I R N N M
U L D R V Q Z I I L B K O J S T R L Q M
S Y E T A R T S O R P P O N D E R O U S
H P D C B R O S U N W C L H G F M U I L
Y W R W V X N U S Y L T S A H G C S L J
Q I H L G O X C S E T T E N O I R A M M
D B S C C E L B A T I M O D N I Q N H G
```

annoying; irritating (7)
bitter; harsh (5)
burden; trial (6)
bustling; swarming (7)
calm; peaceful (8)
calmly (8)
comfortingly; soothingly (11)
confidence: self-___ (9)
crossness; irritability (9)
danger (5)
dangerous (8)
departure (7)
disapproval of self; self-___ (11)
disgust; distaste (9)
dreadful; horrible (7)
dull; dreary (9)
ecstatic; thrilled (8)
elegant; rich (9)
every which way; no pattern: helter-___ (7)
giant; huge (7)
hanging structure (7)
heavy; stifling (10)
jealous; resentful (7)

lessened; subsided (7)
limitless (8)
look (6)
minister; preacher (6)
miserable; forsaken (7)
mournful; pitiful (6)
pain; suffering (7)
partner; accessory (10)
partnership (7)
pleasing; charming (9)
puppet (10)
skimpy; sparse (6)
sleepy; cow-like (6)
supreme; unconquerable (11)
thrilled ; overjoyed (6)
to bring out of a state of sleep (5)
uncontrollably (10)
unlearned; ignorant people (11)
without regret (11)
worn out; exhausted (9)

Tuck Everlasting Vocabulary Word Search 2 Answer Key

Words are placed backwards, forward, diagonally, up and down. Clues listed below can help you find the words. Circle the hidden vocabulary words in the maze.

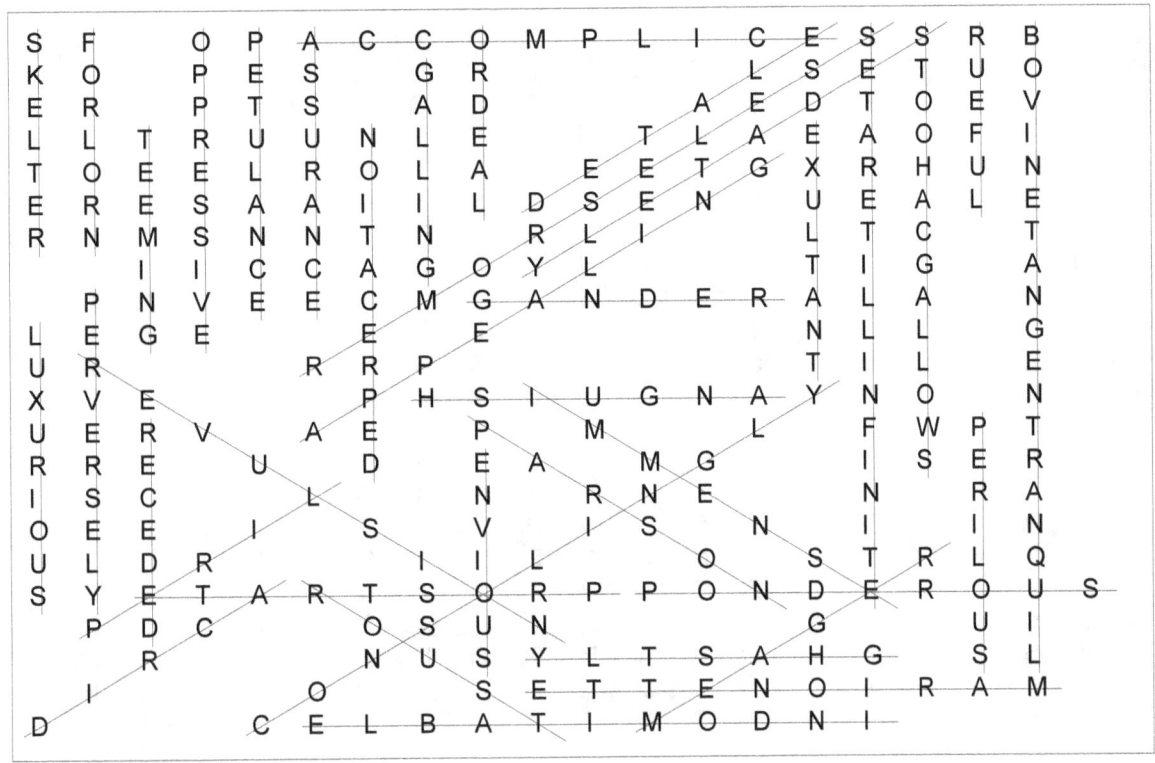

annoying; irritating (7)
bitter; harsh (5)
burden; trial (6)
bustling; swarming (7)
calm; peaceful (8)
calmly (8)
comfortingly; soothingly (11)
confidence: self-___ (9)
crossness; irritability (9)
danger (5)
dangerous (8)
departure (7)
disapproval of self; self-___ (11)
disgust; distaste (9)
dreadful; horrible (7)
dull; dreary (9)
ecstatic; thrilled (8)
elegant; rich (9)
every which way; no pattern: helter-___ (7)
giant; huge (7)
hanging structure (7)
heavy; stifling (10)
jealous; resentful (7)

lessened; subsided (7)
limitless (8)
look (6)
minister; preacher (6)
miserable; forsaken (7)
mournful; pitiful (6)
pain; suffering (7)
partner; accessory (10)
partnership (7)
pleasing; charming (9)
puppet (10)
skimpy; sparse (6)
sleepy; cow-like (6)
supreme; unconquerable (11)
thrilled ; overjoyed (6)
to bring out of a state of sleep (5)
uncontrollably (10)
unlearned; ignorant people (11)
without regret (11)
worn out; exhausted (9)

Tuck Everlasting Vocabulary Word Search 3

Words are placed backwards, forward, diagonally, up and down. Words listed below are included in the maze. Circle the hidden vocabulary words in the maze.

```
C O N S O L I N G L Y D K Y M H G P A S
M D Z T P R E C E D E D P F E N P R N Y
B A R B A R I A N T S S F Q L Z S O G L
C F D S R E C N A L U T E P A X C G U T
I F V U S Y Z L Y O O F L T N D M T I N
N N M O O E E V R B I K R K C T S R S A
F T F L N Y W E K S V A W R H W Y A H V
Q M Q I F G D Y R A N I D R O A R T X E
Y N V R N V J H Q E Q Q L L U E E V L
F O M E O I X Y U P S R L T Y E S I E E
B I E P D L T I A G G A S S M D S T X R
G T T R E A L E S B G U V I I S Q X U R
H A A E C E X F S Y O Q N R E J Y O L I
A C P V I P S Z U I L G C R C F R M T C
S E H U S P R T R S E A P X G D L E A X
T R Y L I A W U A S K P T N E U I A N T
L P S S V G X Q N U O E I A F Z R G T H
Y E I I E U A E C P N L L E N Q E E V R
W D C O L R M N E M L C U T P G P R S K
Z V S N Y M G W D A R R H L E V E J X J
G N I L I A L F G E F O R L O R N N Q M
S U B M I S S I O N R D Z D Y Z C F T K
```

ACRID	EXTRAORDINARY	LUXURIOUS	PROSTRATE
ANGUISH	EXULTANT	MEAGER	RECEDED
APPEALING	FLAILING	MELANCHOLY	REVULSION
ASSURANCE	FORLORN	METAPHYSICS	ROUST
BARBARIAN	GALLING	OPPRESSIVE	RUEFUL
BOVINE	GALLOWS	ORDEAL	SKELTER
CONSOLINGLY	GANDER	PARSON	STAUNCHLY
DECISIVELY	GHASTLY	PERIL	SUBMISSION
DEPRECATION	IMMENSE	PERILOUS	TANGENT
ELATED	INFINITE	PETULANCE	TEEMING
ENVIOUS	IRRELEVANTLY	PONDEROUS	TRANQUIL

Tuck Everlasting Vocabulary Word Search 3 Answer Key

Words are placed backwards, forward, diagonally, up and down. Words listed below are included in the maze. Circle the hidden vocabulary words in the maze.

ACRID	EXTRAORDINARY	LUXURIOUS	PROSTRATE
ANGUISH	EXULTANT	MEAGER	RECEDED
APPEALING	FLAILING	MELANCHOLY	REVULSION
ASSURANCE	FORLORN	METAPHYSICS	ROUST
BARBARIAN	GALLING	OPPRESSIVE	RUEFUL
BOVINE	GALLOWS	ORDEAL	SKELTER
CONSOLINGLY	GANDER	PARSON	STAUNCHLY
DECISIVELY	GHASTLY	PERIL	SUBMISSION
DEPRECATION	IMMENSE	PERILOUS	TANGENT
ELATED	INFINITE	PETULANCE	TEEMING
ENVIOUS	IRRELEVANTLY	PONDEROUS	TRANQUIL

Tuck Everlasting Vocabulary Word Search 4

Words are placed backwards, forward, diagonally, up and down. Words listed below are included in the maze. Circle the hidden vocabulary words in the maze.

```
P L A I N T I V E L Y L T S A H G L N W
L E R B M T F H N F W Y P G P Y A V B N
G G R E M D F L Z T R A M A E P B N D
Y A N I V V E A L I W Y R A D L M P V P
L J L P L U I N L V L F S R Y D L T V V
E W N L E L L I S R Q E O I L S M O H N
V R F N I T T S K E T Y N O D B N L W M
I S Z N R N U Y I A L L Y N E A G X F S
S K G P E O G L R O Q T M E T R L E R
I E D G L L T E A Y N N D T C B F T T F
C L M I X V T T N N L A D T A A A W G Y
E T R E Y I Y A Y L C V R E R R B H X Z
D E T A L E Z D E P R E C A T I O N H Y
P R Z L E A X E R Y M L S S S A D S R K
F T I A S P N S M O C E O W I N I K E Y
O A C C R P W C R S X R B Z D U T G C R
R N A R E E P S H U P R R O G A N D E R
L G H I V A E R L O E I O N V I L G D Z
O E O D R L S T V I L F A U M I A P E B
R N N O M E I A G D V V Y U E S E N S D S
N T T S P N C K R N Q L E L M T H E F T
C T S D T G K P G E V T R A N Q U I L F
```

ACRID   ELATED   GHASTLY   PERIL   ROUST

ANGUISH   ENVIOUS   ILLITERATES   PERILOUS   RUEFUL

APPEALING   EXULTANT   IMMENSE   PERVERSELY   SEDATELY

BARBARIAN   FLAILING   IRRELEVANTLY   PETULANCE   SKELTER

BOVINE   FORLORN   MARIONETTE   PLAINTIVELY   TANGENT

CAHOOTS   GALLING   MEAGER   PROSTRATE   TEEMING

DECISIVELY   GALLOWS   MELANCHOLY   RECEDED   TRANQUIL

DEPRECATION   GANDER   ORDEAL   REMORSELESS

DISTRACTEDLY   GENTILITY   PARSON   REVULSION

Tuck Everlasting Vocabulary Word Search 4 Answer Key

Words are placed backwards, forward, diagonally, up and down. Words listed below are included in the maze. Circle the hidden vocabulary words in the maze.

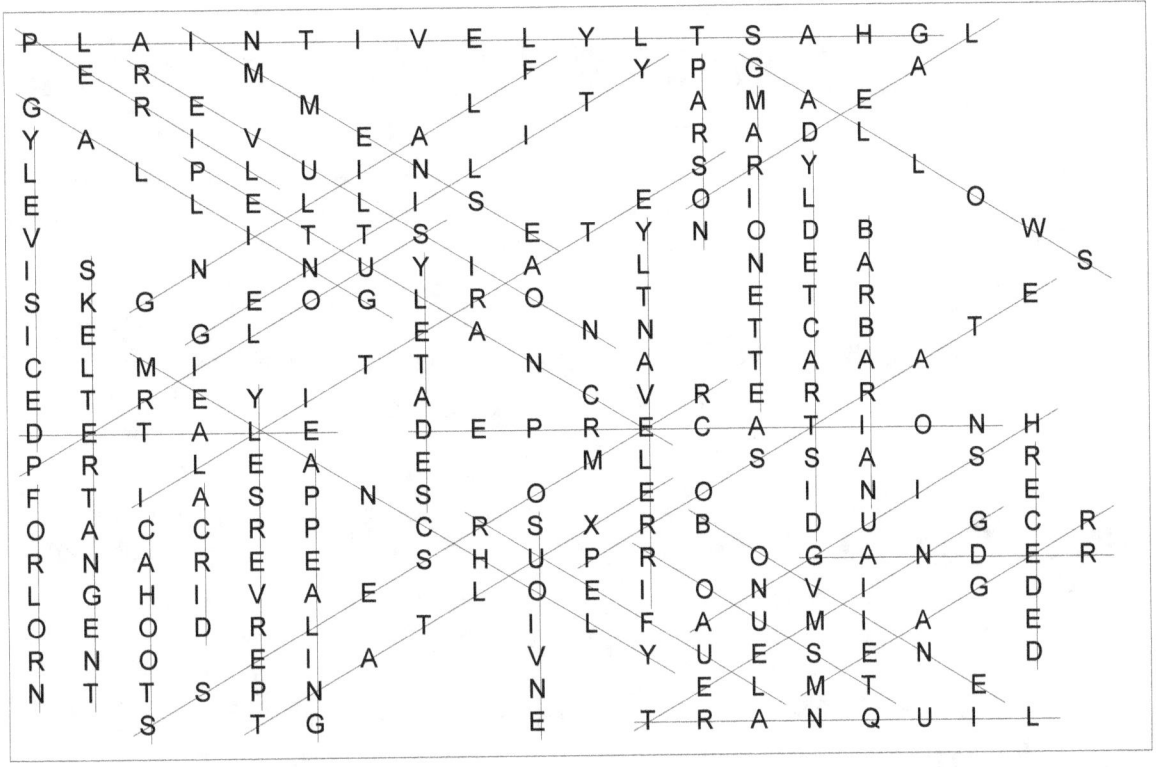

ACRID	ELATED	GHASTLY	PERIL	ROUST
ANGUISH	ENVIOUS	ILLITERATES	PERILOUS	RUEFUL
APPEALING	EXULTANT	IMMENSE	PERVERSELY	SEDATELY
BARBARIAN	FLAILING	IRRELEVANTLY	PETULANCE	SKELTER
BOVINE	FORLORN	MARIONETTE	PLAINTIVELY	TANGENT
CAHOOTS	GALLING	MEAGER	PROSTRATE	TEEMING
DECISIVELY	GALLOWS	MELANCHOLY	RECEDED	TRANQUIL
DEPRECATION	GANDER	ORDEAL	REMORSELESS	
DISTRACTEDLY	GENTILITY	PARSON	REVULSION	

Tuck Everlasting Vocabulary Crossword 1

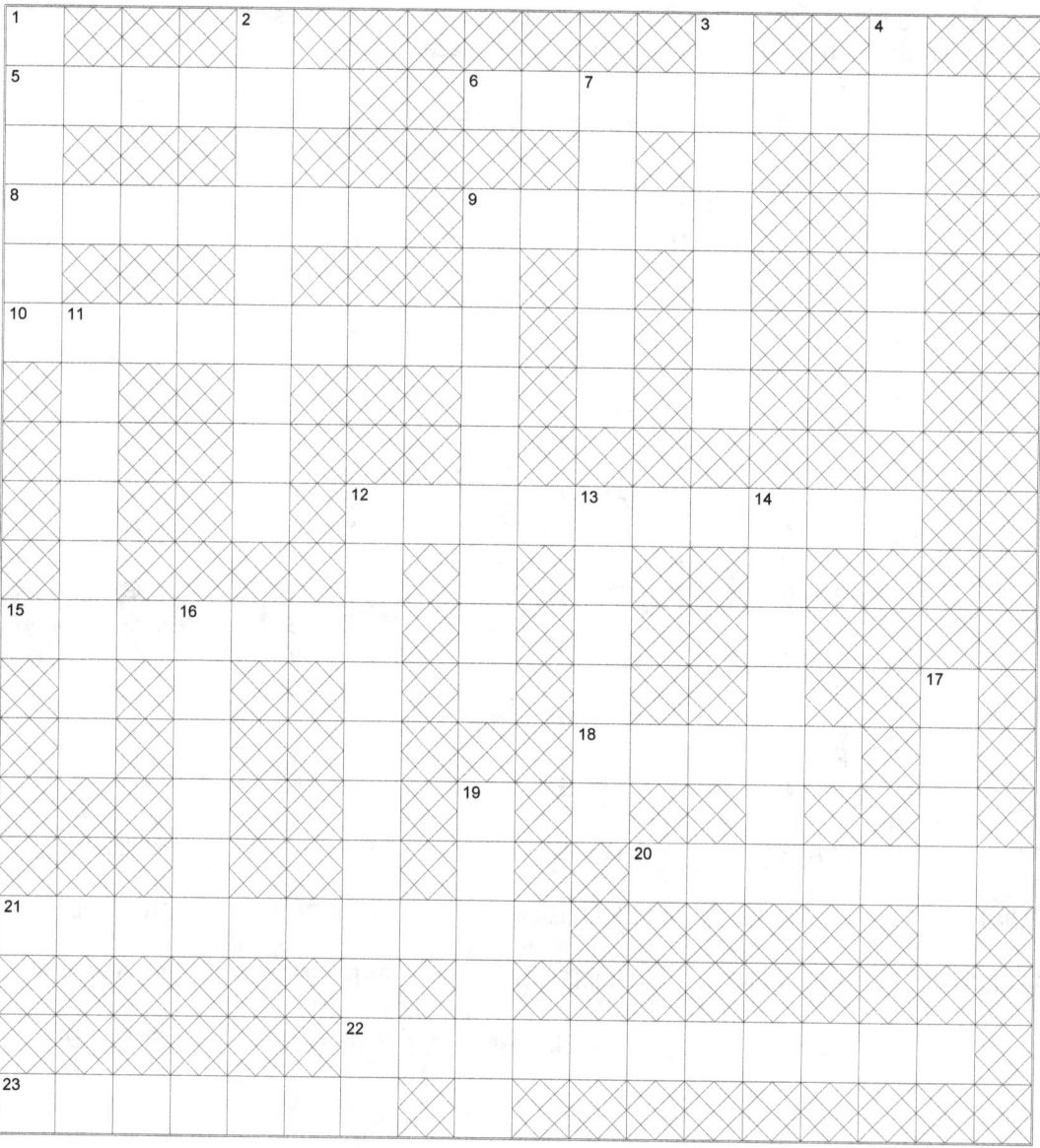

Across
5. thrilled ; overjoyed
6. pleasing; charming
8. dreadful; horrible
9. danger
10. disgust; distaste
12. puppet
15. departure
18. bitter; harsh
20. pain; suffering
21. heavy; stifling
22. comfortingly; soothingly
23. partnership

Down
1. skimpy; sparse
2. elegance; grace
3. annoying; irritating
4. jealous; resentful
7. minister; preacher
9. dull; dreary
11. ecstatic; thrilled
12. branch of science
13. burden; trial
14. bustling; swarming
16. look
17. to bring out of a state of sleep
19. sleepy; cow-like

Tuck Everlasting Vocabulary Crossword 1 Answer Key

Across
5. thrilled ; overjoyed
6. pleasing; charming
8. dreadful; horrible
9. danger
10. disgust; distaste
12. puppet
15. departure
18. bitter; harsh
20. pain; suffering
21. heavy; stifling
22. comfortingly; soothingly
23. partnership

Down
1. skimpy; sparse
2. elegance; grace
3. annoying; irritating
4. jealous; resentful
7. minister; preacher
9. dull; dreary
11. ecstatic; thrilled
12. branch of science
13. burden; trial
14. bustling; swarming
16. look
17. to bring out of a state of sleep
19. sleepy; cow-like

Tuck Everlasting Vocabulary Crossword 2

Across
3. jealous; resentful
5. miserable; forsaken
7. gloomy; woeful
10. thrilled ; overjoyed
12. danger
13. look
16. calm; peaceful
17. bitter; harsh
19. dangerous
20. limitless
21. hanging structure
22. pain; suffering

Down
1. branch of science
2. obedience; meekness
4. giant; huge
5. thrashing
6. lessened; subsided
8. burden; trial
9. bustling; swarming
11. confidence: self-___
12. crossness; irritability
14. pleasing; charming
15. calmly
18. to bring out of a state of sleep

Tuck Everlasting Vocabulary Crossword 2 Answer Key

Across
- 3. jealous; resentful
- 5. miserable; forsaken
- 7. gloomy; woeful
- 10. thrilled ; overjoyed
- 12. danger
- 13. look
- 16. calm; peaceful
- 17. bitter; harsh
- 19. dangerous
- 20. limitless
- 21. hanging structure
- 22. pain; suffering

Down
- 1. branch of science
- 2. obedience; meekness
- 4. giant; huge
- 5. thrashing
- 6. lessened; subsided
- 8. burden; trial
- 9. bustling; swarming
- 11. confidence: self-___
- 12. crossness; irritability
- 14. pleasing; charming
- 15. calmly
- 18. to bring out of a state of sleep

Tuck Everlasting Vocabulary Crossword 3

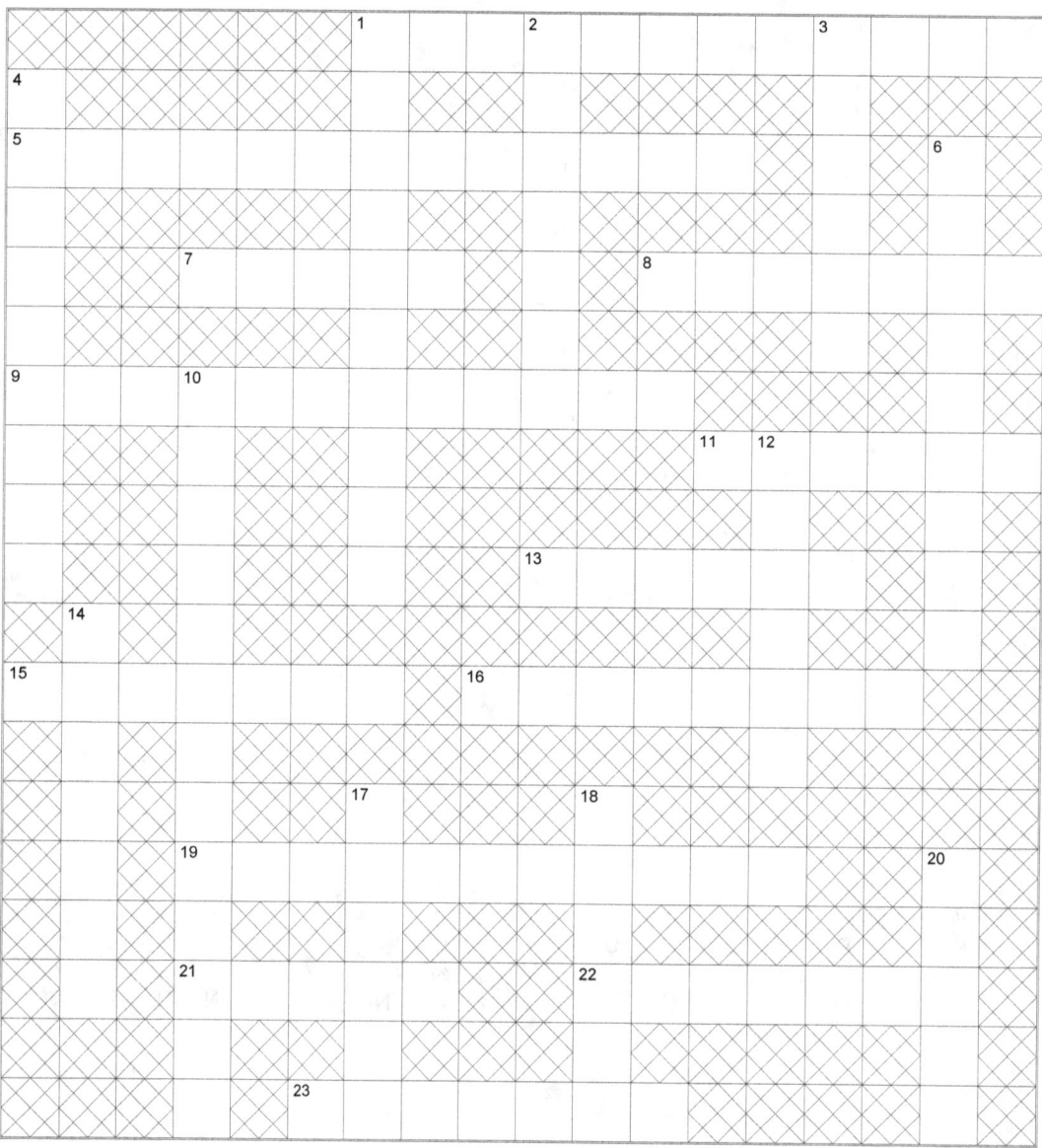

Across
1. in bewilderment; confusedly
5. unafraid; not hesitant
7. to bring out of a state of sleep
8. giant; huge
9. in a 'beside the point' manner
11. burden; trial
13. look
15. partnership
16. calm; peaceful
19. supreme; unconquerable
21. bitter; harsh
22. every which way; no pattern: helter-___
23. bustling; swarming

Down
1. with determination
2. departure
3. thrilled ; overjoyed
4. elegant; rich
6. confidence: self-___
10. amazing; remarkable
12. mournful; pitiful
14. hanging structure
17. sleepy; cow-like
18. minister; preacher
20. danger

Tuck Everlasting Vocabulary Crossword 3 Answer Key

Across
1. in bewilderment; confusedly
5. unafraid; not hesitant
7. to bring out of a state of sleep
8. giant; huge
9. in a 'beside the point' manner
11. burden; trial
13. look
15. partnership
16. calm; peaceful
19. supreme; unconquerable
21. bitter; harsh
22. every which way; no pattern: helter-___
23. bustling; swarming

Down
1. with determination
2. departure
3. thrilled; overjoyed
4. elegant; rich
6. confidence: self-___
10. amazing; remarkable
12. mournful; pitiful
14. hanging structure
17. sleepy; cow-like
18. minister; preacher
20. danger

Tuck Everlasting Vocabulary Crossword 4

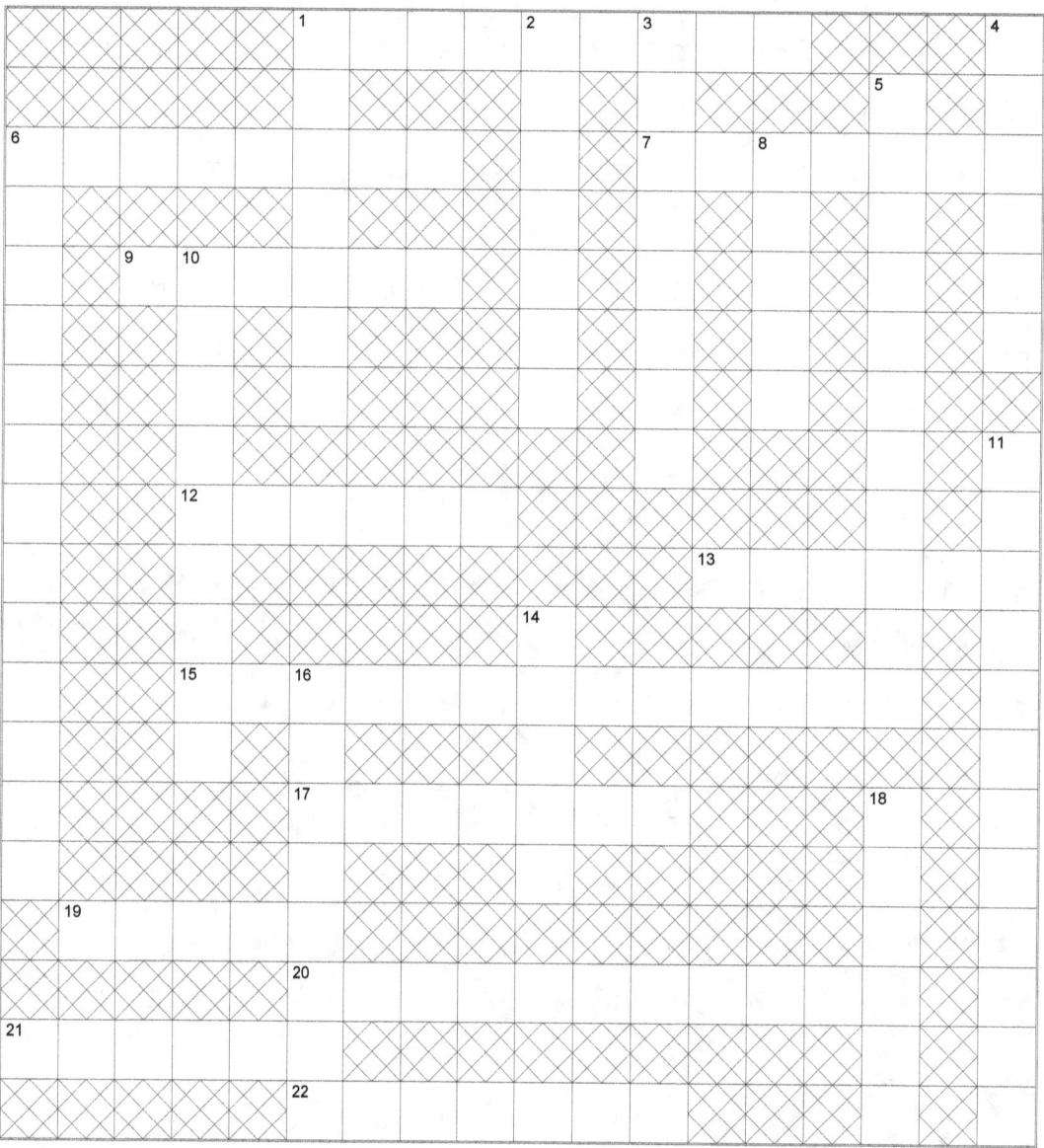

Across
1. elegance; grace
6. ecstatic; thrilled
7. miserable; forsaken
9. thrilled ; overjoyed
12. mournful; pitiful
13. skimpy; sparse
15. unafraid; not hesitant
17. pain; suffering
19. danger
20. supreme; unconquerable
21. minister; preacher
22. hanging structure

Down
1. dreadful; horrible
2. giant; huge
3. limitless
4. look
5. comfortingly; soothingly
6. amazing; remarkable
8. to bring out of a state of sleep
10. elegant; rich
11. in a 'beside the point' manner
14. bitter; harsh
16. thrashing
18. burden; trial

Tuck Everlasting Vocabulary Crossword 4 Answer Key

Across
1. elegance; grace
6. ecstatic; thrilled
7. miserable; forsaken
9. thrilled ; overjoyed
12. mournful; pitiful
13. skimpy; sparse
15. unafraid; not hesitant
17. pain; suffering
19. danger
20. supreme; unconquerable
21. minister; preacher
22. hanging structure

Down
1. dreadful; horrible
2. giant; huge
3. limitless
4. look
5. comfortingly; soothingly
6. amazing; remarkable
8. to bring out of a state of sleep
10. elegant; rich
11. in a 'beside the point' manner
14. bitter; harsh
16. thrashing
18. burden; trial

Tuck Everlasting Vocabulary Juggle Letters 1

1. INEUOSV = 1. _____
   jealous; resentful

2. NAMBITDOLIE = 2. _____
   supreme; unconquerable

3. IOSNSMSUIB = 3. _____
   obedience; meekness

4. HTOACOS = 4. _____
   partnership

5. SONPRA = 5. _____
   minister; preacher

6. IOLSURNEV = 6. _____
   disgust; distaste

7. TLSAETLIERI = 7. _____
   unlearned; ignorant people

8. ORSTPRAET = 8. _____
   worn out; exhausted

9. EESTYDLA = 9. _____
   calmly

10. ASULTNYCH =10. _____
    loyally; faithfully

11. BARBNARIA =11. _____
    savage; brute

12. EAUTPLECN =12. _____
    crossness; irritability

13. AOEYROLVRTINU =13. _____
    rebellious; unique

14. LXEUATTN =14. _____
    ecstatic; thrilled

15. VAEUCSRNO =15. _____
    hollow and deep sounding

Tuck Everlasting Vocabulary Juggle Letters 1 Answer Key

1. INEUOSV = 1. ENVIOUS
jealous; resentful

2. NAMBITDOLIE = 2. INDOMITABLE
supreme; unconquerable

3. IOSNSMSUIB = 3. SUBMISSION
obedience; meekness

4. HTOACOS = 4. CAHOOTS
partnership

5. SONPRA = 5. PARSON
minister; preacher

6. IOLSURNEV = 6. REVULSION
disgust; distaste

7. TLSAETLIERI = 7. ILLITERATES
unlearned; ignorant people

8. ORSTPRAET = 8. PROSTRATE
worn out; exhausted

9. EESTYDLA = 9. SEDATELY
calmly

10. ASULTNYCH =10. STAUNCHLY
loyally; faithfully

11. BARBNARIA =11. BARBARIAN
savage; brute

12. EAUTPLECN =12. PETULANCE
crossness; irritability

13. AOEYROLVRTINU =13. REVOLUTIONARY
rebellious; unique

14. LXEUATTN =14. EXULTANT
ecstatic; thrilled

15. VAEUCSRNO =15. CAVERNOUS
hollow and deep sounding

Tuck Everlasting Vocabulary Juggle Letters 2

1. IAHUNSG = 1. _____
   pain; suffering

2. CEREDED = 2. _____
   lessened; subsided

3. SLGWAOL = 3. _____
   hanging structure

4. SPNORA = 4. _____
   minister; preacher

5. OCMDTNCOSIMAOA = 5. _____
   lodging

6. REEPVYELRS = 6. _____
   uncontrollably

7. NTTGIILYE = 7. _____
   elegance; grace

8. NGPPEAALI = 8. _____
   pleasing; charming

9. ORLRESEESSM = 9. _____
   without regret

10. IBNRABARA = 10. _____
    savage; brute

11. TININIFE = 11. _____
    limitless

12. OCCLPAIMCE = 12. _____
    partner; accessory

13. ERTPCEODIAN = 13. _____
    disapproval of self; self-___

14. RIPUEOSL = 14. _____
    dangerous

15. INLFLAIG = 15. _____
    thrashing

Tuck Everlasting Vocabulary Juggle Letters 2 Answer Key

1. IAHUNSG = 1. ANGUISH
   pain; suffering

2. CEREDED = 2. RECEDED
   lessened; subsided

3. SLGWAOL = 3. GALLOWS
   hanging structure

4. SPNORA = 4. PARSON
   minister; preacher

5. OCMDTNCOSIMAOA = 5. ACCOMMODATIONS
   lodging

6. REEPVYELRS = 6. PERVERSELY
   uncontrollably

7. NTTGIILYE = 7. GENTILITY
   elegance; grace

8. NGPPEAALI = 8. APPEALING
   pleasing; charming

9. ORLRESEESSM = 9. REMORSELESS
   without regret

10. IBNRABARA = 10. BARBARIAN
    savage; brute

11. TININIFE = 11. INFINITE
    limitless

12. OCCLPAIMCE = 12. ACCOMPLICE
    partner; accessory

13. ERTPCEODIAN = 13. DEPRECATION
    disapproval of self; self-____

14. RIPUEOSL = 14. PERILOUS
    dangerous

15. INLFLAIG = 15. FLAILING
    thrashing

Tuck Everlasting Vocabulary Juggle Letters 3

1. IGLLGNA = 1. _____
   annoying; irritating

2. LASNHYUCT = 2. _____
   loyally; faithfully

3. UURFEL = 3. _____
   mournful; pitiful

4. HSPATIMSCEY = 4. _____
   branch of science

5. EPAETCULN = 5. _____
   crossness; irritability

6. GNNATTE = 6. _____
   departure

7. RVYESEPREL = 7. _____
   uncontrollably

8. SOTHAOC = 8. _____
   partnership

9. RPOSAN = 9. _____
   minister; preacher

10. EADROL =10. _____
    burden; trial

11. YITETLNIG =11. _____
    elegance; grace

12. EDAELT =12. _____
    thrilled ; overjoyed

13. FLORONR =13. _____
    miserable; forsaken

14. LINNLGYNIFHUC =14. _____
    unafraid; not hesitant

15. ODTACIMONOMCSA =15. _____
    lodging

Tuck Everlasting Vocabulary Juggle Letters 3 Answer Key

1. IGLLGNA = 1. GALLING
   annoying; irritating

2. LASNHYUCT = 2. STAUNCHLY
   loyally; faithfully

3. UURFEL = 3. RUEFUL
   mournful; pitiful

4. HSPATIMSCEY = 4. METAPHYSICS
   branch of science

5. EPAETCULN = 5. PETULANCE
   crossness; irritability

6. GNNATTE = 6. TANGENT
   departure

7. RVYESEPREL = 7. PERVERSELY
   uncontrollably

8. SOTHAOC = 8. CAHOOTS
   partnership

9. RPOSAN = 9. PARSON
   minister; preacher

10. EADROL = 10. ORDEAL
    burden; trial

11. YITETLNIG = 11. GENTILITY
    elegance; grace

12. EDAELT = 12. ELATED
    thrilled ; overjoyed

13. FLORONR = 13. FORLORN
    miserable; forsaken

14. LINNLGYNIFHUC = 14. UNFLINCHINGLY
    unafraid; not hesitant

15. ODTACIMONOMCSA = 15. ACCOMMODATIONS
    lodging

Tuck Everlasting Vocabulary Juggle Letters 4

1. OTYINVLRAEORU = 1. _____
   rebellious; unique

2. CUSAERNAS = 2. _____
   confidence: self-___

3. IARDC = 3. _____
   bitter; harsh

4. VBONEI = 4. _____
   sleepy; cow-like

5. LGAGNLI = 5. _____
   annoying; irritating

6. ISTRDDCAYTLE = 6. _____
   in bewilderment; confusedly

7. GASIUNH = 7. _____
   pain; suffering

8. INVEOULSR = 8. _____
   disgust; distaste

9. UEFRUL = 9. _____
   mournful; pitiful

10. LOIPACCMCE = 10. _____
    partner; accessory

11. EDRDEEC = 11. _____
    lessened; subsided

12. COMCIMTNOAOSAD = 12. _____
    lodging

13. ETGEINM = 13. _____
    bustling; swarming

14. NREAGD = 14. _____
    look

15. AEENTRPIDOC = 15. _____
    disapproval of self; self-___

Tuck Everlasting Vocabulary Juggle Letters 4 Answer Key

1. OTYINVLRAEORU = 1. REVOLUTIONARY
   rebellious; unique

2. CUSAERNAS = 2. ASSURANCE
   confidence: self-___

3. IARDC = 3. ACRID
   bitter; harsh

4. VBONEI = 4. BOVINE
   sleepy; cow-like

5. LGAGNLI = 5. GALLING
   annoying; irritating

6. ISTRDDCAYTLE = 6. DISTRACTEDLY
   in bewilderment; confusedly

7. GASIUNH = 7. ANGUISH
   pain; suffering

8. INVEOULSR = 8. REVULSION
   disgust; distaste

9. UEFRUL = 9. RUEFUL
   mournful; pitiful

10. LOIPACCMCE = 10. ACCOMPLICE
    partner; accessory

11. EDRDEEC = 11. RECEDED
    lessened; subsided

12. COMCIMTNOAOSAD = 12. ACCOMMODATIONS
    lodging

13. ETGEINM = 13. TEEMING
    bustling; swarming

14. NREAGD = 14. GANDER
    look

15. AEENTRPIDOC = 15. DEPRECATION
    disapproval of self; self-___

ACCOMMODATIONS	lodging
ACCOMPLICE	partner; accessory
ACRID	bitter; harsh
ANGUISH	pain; suffering
APPEALING	pleasing; charming
ASSURANCE	confidence: self-___

BARBARIAN	savage; brute
BOVINE	sleepy; cow-like
CAHOOTS	partnership
CAVERNOUS	hollow and deep sounding
CONSOLINGLY	comfortingly; soothingly
DECISIVELY	with determination

DEPRECATION	disapproval of self; self-___
DISTRACTEDLY	in bewilderment; confusedly
ELATED	thrilled ; overjoyed
ENVIOUS	jealous; resentful
EXTRAORDINARY	amazing; remarkable
EXULTANT	ecstatic; thrilled

FLAILING	thrashing
FORLORN	miserable; forsaken
GALLING	annoying; irritating
GALLOWS	hanging structure
GANDER	look
GENTILITY	elegance; grace

GHASTLY	dreadful; horrible
ILLITERATES	unlearned; ignorant people
IMMENSE	giant; huge
INDOMITABLE	supreme; unconquerable
INFINITE	limitless
IRRELEVANTLY	in a 'beside the point' manner

LUXURIOUS	elegant; rich
MARIONETTE	puppet
MEAGER	skimpy; sparse
MELANCHOLY	gloomy; woeful
METAPHYSICS	branch of science
OPPRESSIVE	heavy; stifling

ORDEAL	burden; trial
PARSON	minister; preacher
PERIL	danger
PERILOUS	dangerous
PERVERSELY	uncontrollably
PETULANCE	crossness; irritability

PLAINTIVELY	sorrowfully
PONDEROUS	dull; dreary
PROSTRATE	worn out; exhausted
RECEDED	lessened; subsided
REMORSELESS	without regret
REVOLUTIONARY	rebellious; unique

REVULSION	disgust; distaste
ROUST	to bring out of a state of sleep
RUEFUL	mournful; pitiful
SEDATELY	calmly
SKELTER	every which way; no pattern: helter-___
STAUNCHLY	loyally; faithfully

SUBMISSION	obedience; meekness
TANGENT	departure
TEEMING	bustling; swarming
TRANQUIL	calm; peaceful
UNFLINCHINGLY	unafraid; not hesitant

Tuck Everlasting Vocabulary

ILLITERATES	MELANCHOLY	GALLOWS	TANGENT	GALLING
MEAGER	CONSOLINGLY	ACCOMMODATIONS	GANDER	BOVINE
PROSTRATE	BARBARIAN	FREE SPACE	RUEFUL	GENTILITY
INFINITE	REMORSELESS	PLAINTIVELY	ENVIOUS	SKELTER
ELATED	DISTRACTEDLY	DEPRECATION	METAPHYSICS	PERILOUS

Tuck Everlasting Vocabulary

APPEALING	PARSON	ORDEAL	PETULANCE	LUXURIOUS
ANGUISH	ASSURANCE	EXULTANT	CAHOOTS	INDOMITABLE
GHASTLY	CAVERNOUS	FREE SPACE	ACCOMPLICE	PERVERSELY
PERIL	ACRID	SEDATELY	MARIONETTE	UNFLINCHINGLY
TEEMING	SUBMISSION	DECISIVELY	EXTRAORDINARY	IMMENSE

Tuck Everlasting Vocabulary

ANGUISH	LUXURIOUS	CONSOLINGLY	PERIL	TEEMING
MELANCHOLY	IRRELEVANTLY	BOVINE	ACCOMMODATIONS	IMMENSE
DECISIVELY	ELATED	FREE SPACE	GALLING	PLAINTIVELY
GANDER	TRANQUIL	ORDEAL	ACCOMPLICE	CAVERNOUS
RUEFUL	REVULSION	CAHOOTS	DEPRECATION	STAUNCHLY

Tuck Everlasting Vocabulary

ACRID	GENTILITY	ENVIOUS	PONDEROUS	METAPHYSICS
EXTRAORDINARY	GALLOWS	PERILOUS	RECEDED	BARBARIAN
FORLORN	ROUST	FREE SPACE	FLAILING	INFINITE
PROSTRATE	ILLITERATES	PETULANCE	MEAGER	REVOLUTIONARY
DISTRACTEDLY	SUBMISSION	GHASTLY	TANGENT	MARIONETTE

Tuck Everlasting Vocabulary

RECEDED	REVOLUTIONARY	INFINITE	PONDEROUS	FLAILING
EXTRAORDINARY	ACCOMPLICE	SKELTER	GHASTLY	PERILOUS
INDOMITABLE	REVULSION	FREE SPACE	REMORSELESS	TANGENT
ROUST	SEDATELY	RUEFUL	IRRELEVANTLY	UNFLINCHINGLY
ACCOMMODATIONS	CAHOOTS	ASSURANCE	SUBMISSION	OPPRESSIVE

Tuck Everlasting Vocabulary

CAVERNOUS	DISTRACTEDLY	ORDEAL	TRANQUIL	GANDER
ENVIOUS	MARIONETTE	IMMENSE	TEEMING	EXULTANT
PARSON	BARBARIAN	FREE SPACE	MELANCHOLY	BOVINE
APPEALING	PROSTRATE	ANGUISH	ELATED	MEAGER
GALLING	GENTILITY	ILLITERATES	DECISIVELY	DEPRECATION

Tuck Everlasting Vocabulary

BOVINE	FLAILING	PARSON	ANGUISH	PERIL
PETULANCE	EXULTANT	FORLORN	ROUST	GHASTLY
EXTRAORDINARY	GENTILITY	FREE SPACE	RUEFUL	ACCOMPLICE
REVOLUTIONARY	LUXURIOUS	INDOMITABLE	IRRELEVANTLY	GANDER
PLAINTIVELY	REVULSION	ORDEAL	SUBMISSION	PROSTRATE

Tuck Everlasting Vocabulary

STAUNCHLY	TEEMING	OPPRESSIVE	ACRID	ACCOMMODATIONS
IMMENSE	MEAGER	PONDEROUS	PERVERSELY	MELANCHOLY
ILLITERATES	ENVIOUS	FREE SPACE	UNFLINCHINGLY	APPEALING
TANGENT	INFINITE	DECISIVELY	SEDATELY	MARIONETTE
CAHOOTS	GALLING	CONSOLINGLY	PERILOUS	ELATED

Tuck Everlasting Vocabulary

REVOLUTIONARY	ASSURANCE	ORDEAL	ROUST	ACRID
TEEMING	SEDATELY	BOVINE	SKELTER	ACCOMMODATIONS
RUEFUL	PARSON	FREE SPACE	PONDEROUS	MEAGER
ANGUISH	ENVIOUS	TANGENT	TRANQUIL	BARBARIAN
LUXURIOUS	DEPRECATION	GENTILITY	RECEDED	IRRELEVANTLY

Tuck Everlasting Vocabulary

ACCOMPLICE	PERILOUS	DISTRACTEDLY	GHASTLY	DECISIVELY
PERIL	ILLITERATES	GALLING	PROSTRATE	INFINITE
GALLOWS	SUBMISSION	FREE SPACE	PLAINTIVELY	EXULTANT
MARIONETTE	INDOMITABLE	STAUNCHLY	FORLORN	REMORSELESS
PETULANCE	REVULSION	IMMENSE	UNFLINCHINGLY	CONSOLINGLY

Tuck Everlasting Vocabulary

TANGENT	EXTRAORDINARY	IMMENSE	FORLORN	DECISIVELY
FLAILING	MELANCHOLY	ANGUISH	BOVINE	TRANQUIL
GANDER	CAVERNOUS	FREE SPACE	RECEDED	CAHOOTS
PARSON	UNFLINCHINGLY	EXULTANT	PERIL	PERVERSELY
DEPRECATION	INFINITE	ORDEAL	ENVIOUS	OPPRESSIVE

Tuck Everlasting Vocabulary

DISTRACTEDLY	GHASTLY	PERILOUS	GENTILITY	GALLING
ACCOMPLICE	STAUNCHLY	SKELTER	ILLITERATES	PETULANCE
SUBMISSION	ACCOMMODATIONS	FREE SPACE	REMORSELESS	PLAINTIVELY
GALLOWS	PONDEROUS	REVOLUTIONARY	BARBARIAN	CONSOLINGLY
PROSTRATE	MARIONETTE	METAPHYSICS	INDOMITABLE	MEAGER

Tuck Everlasting Vocabulary

IRRELEVANTLY	INFINITE	GALLING	GHASTLY	REMORSELESS
DISTRACTEDLY	MEAGER	PETULANCE	PERVERSELY	SEDATELY
METAPHYSICS	TEEMING	FREE SPACE	REVULSION	GALLOWS
ASSURANCE	ACCOMPLICE	ELATED	DEPRECATION	ROUST
LUXURIOUS	MELANCHOLY	TANGENT	FLAILING	SKELTER

Tuck Everlasting Vocabulary

PROSTRATE	UNFLINCHINGLY	TRANQUIL	PARSON	EXULTANT
PERIL	GANDER	CAVERNOUS	ORDEAL	RUEFUL
BOVINE	MARIONETTE	FREE SPACE	GENTILITY	INDOMITABLE
IMMENSE	ILLITERATES	FORLORN	ENVIOUS	APPEALING
ACRID	DECISIVELY	STAUNCHLY	RECEDED	ANGUISH

Tuck Everlasting Vocabulary

BOVINE	PETULANCE	EXTRAORDINARY	REMORSELESS	ROUST
PARSON	SEDATELY	ORDEAL	GALLOWS	ACCOMMODATIONS
PERIL	GHASTLY	FREE SPACE	ACRID	PERILOUS
DECISIVELY	PERVERSELY	CAHOOTS	PROSTRATE	ILLITERATES
FORLORN	GANDER	ASSURANCE	TRANQUIL	CONSOLINGLY

Tuck Everlasting Vocabulary

LUXURIOUS	UNFLINCHINGLY	DISTRACTEDLY	MARIONETTE	MEAGER
ELATED	ACCOMPLICE	INDOMITABLE	PONDEROUS	PLAINTIVELY
INFINITE	ENVIOUS	FREE SPACE	FLAILING	DEPRECATION
TEEMING	STAUNCHLY	GALLING	IMMENSE	SUBMISSION
TANGENT	RUEFUL	OPPRESSIVE	EXULTANT	GENTILITY

Tuck Everlasting Vocabulary

GALLING	MARIONETTE	TANGENT	CAHOOTS	TRANQUIL
REVOLUTIONARY	APPEALING	METAPHYSICS	INFINITE	PERVERSELY
PROSTRATE	IRRELEVANTLY	FREE SPACE	TEEMING	CONSOLINGLY
OPPRESSIVE	DISTRACTEDLY	ACCOMMODATIONS	ACCOMPLICE	ELATED
MEAGER	GENTILITY	RUEFUL	BARBARIAN	GHASTLY

Tuck Everlasting Vocabulary

SUBMISSION	PERIL	FLAILING	GANDER	ILLITERATES
FORLORN	REMORSELESS	EXTRAORDINARY	RECEDED	ACRID
GALLOWS	ORDEAL	FREE SPACE	SKELTER	PONDEROUS
PETULANCE	PERILOUS	ENVIOUS	ASSURANCE	BOVINE
UNFLINCHINGLY	REVULSION	DECISIVELY	PLAINTIVELY	DEPRECATION

Tuck Everlasting Vocabulary

MEAGER	OPPRESSIVE	GANDER	IMMENSE	FORLORN
FLAILING	INFINITE	TEEMING	EXULTANT	LUXURIOUS
DEPRECATION	ORDEAL	FREE SPACE	PERIL	ILLITERATES
GHASTLY	DECISIVELY	REMORSELESS	GALLOWS	ACCOMPLICE
PONDEROUS	REVOLUTIONARY	CONSOLINGLY	TANGENT	INDOMITABLE

Tuck Everlasting Vocabulary

ROUST	REVULSION	GALLING	MELANCHOLY	ELATED
SKELTER	IRRELEVANTLY	ENVIOUS	UNFLINCHINGLY	PERVERSELY
TRANQUIL	PERILOUS	FREE SPACE	ACRID	ASSURANCE
ACCOMMODATIONS	GENTILITY	CAHOOTS	METAPHYSICS	DISTRACTEDLY
STAUNCHLY	RECEDED	PARSON	SEDATELY	RUEFUL

Tuck Everlasting Vocabulary

PERILOUS	DEPRECATION	CAHOOTS	EXULTANT	ENVIOUS
UNFLINCHINGLY	TANGENT	PARSON	ACCOMMODATIONS	FLAILING
RUEFUL	REVOLUTIONARY	FREE SPACE	GHASTLY	STAUNCHLY
PERIL	DISTRACTEDLY	EXTRAORDINARY	ORDEAL	IMMENSE
CONSOLINGLY	ASSURANCE	REMORSELESS	INFINITE	PERVERSELY

Tuck Everlasting Vocabulary

RECEDED	GANDER	IRRELEVANTLY	BOVINE	LUXURIOUS
PONDEROUS	ACCOMPLICE	FORLORN	APPEALING	SKELTER
METAPHYSICS	MEAGER	FREE SPACE	SUBMISSION	PLAINTIVELY
GALLOWS	TEEMING	CAVERNOUS	MARIONETTE	BARBARIAN
MELANCHOLY	ACRID	ILLITERATES	PROSTRATE	PETULANCE

Tuck Everlasting Vocabulary

SKELTER	EXULTANT	RUEFUL	ENVIOUS	CAVERNOUS
ANGUISH	INDOMITABLE	IRRELEVANTLY	PERILOUS	FORLORN
FLAILING	ORDEAL	FREE SPACE	LUXURIOUS	DECISIVELY
PONDEROUS	BOVINE	METAPHYSICS	PARSON	ELATED
APPEALING	RECEDED	GALLOWS	GANDER	MEAGER

Tuck Everlasting Vocabulary

ACCOMPLICE	REVOLUTIONARY	MELANCHOLY	ACCOMMODATIONS	DISTRACTEDLY
CONSOLINGLY	GHASTLY	PLAINTIVELY	ASSURANCE	SEDATELY
SUBMISSION	REMORSELESS	FREE SPACE	TANGENT	IMMENSE
PETULANCE	GALLING	INFINITE	ILLITERATES	ACRID
PERVERSELY	STAUNCHLY	REVULSION	EXTRAORDINARY	BARBARIAN

Tuck Everlasting Vocabulary

ELATED	UNFLINCHINGLY	SUBMISSION	GENTILITY	CAHOOTS
TANGENT	ILLITERATES	REVULSION	PERILOUS	CONSOLINGLY
MEAGER	METAPHYSICS	FREE SPACE	EXULTANT	MARIONETTE
ACCOMMODATIONS	SEDATELY	DECISIVELY	REVOLUTIONARY	ACCOMPLICE
FORLORN	TRANQUIL	GALLING	DEPRECATION	REMORSELESS

Tuck Everlasting Vocabulary

CAVERNOUS	STAUNCHLY	LUXURIOUS	OPPRESSIVE	PLAINTIVELY
ANGUISH	APPEALING	MELANCHOLY	PERVERSELY	FLAILING
TEEMING	ENVIOUS	FREE SPACE	ORDEAL	GALLOWS
IRRELEVANTLY	BOVINE	DISTRACTEDLY	ROUST	PONDEROUS
IMMENSE	PARSON	EXTRAORDINARY	GHASTLY	INDOMITABLE

Tuck Everlasting Vocabulary

BARBARIAN	STAUNCHLY	OPPRESSIVE	RECEDED	TRANQUIL
INDOMITABLE	CAVERNOUS	FLAILING	DEPRECATION	SEDATELY
MELANCHOLY	TEEMING	FREE SPACE	RUEFUL	PETULANCE
REVULSION	GHASTLY	SKELTER	CAHOOTS	UNFLINCHINGLY
PARSON	INFINITE	ROUST	IRRELEVANTLY	ELATED

Tuck Everlasting Vocabulary

EXULTANT	EXTRAORDINARY	GENTILITY	ILLITERATES	ASSURANCE
MARIONETTE	PERILOUS	MEAGER	SUBMISSION	APPEALING
PONDEROUS	LUXURIOUS	FREE SPACE	ACRID	PERIL
BOVINE	CONSOLINGLY	GANDER	PROSTRATE	IMMENSE
METAPHYSICS	FORLORN	ORDEAL	PERVERSELY	GALLOWS

Tuck Everlasting Vocabulary

MELANCHOLY	CAVERNOUS	GALLING	ROUST	MEAGER
METAPHYSICS	PERVERSELY	SKELTER	APPEALING	REMORSELESS
BOVINE	RECEDED	FREE SPACE	REVULSION	PARSON
IRRELEVANTLY	ANGUISH	IMMENSE	INDOMITABLE	FLAILING
DEPRECATION	ACRID	RUEFUL	CAHOOTS	CONSOLINGLY

Tuck Everlasting Vocabulary

ORDEAL	GANDER	INFINITE	MARIONETTE	STAUNCHLY
PERIL	ASSURANCE	ILLITERATES	TEEMING	ENVIOUS
OPPRESSIVE	PROSTRATE	FREE SPACE	DISTRACTEDLY	ACCOMPLICE
EXTRAORDINARY	GENTILITY	DECISIVELY	PERILOUS	GHASTLY
LUXURIOUS	TRANQUIL	GALLOWS	PONDEROUS	TANGENT

Tuck Everlasting Vocabulary

PERVERSELY	ELATED	ANGUISH	PONDEROUS	CAHOOTS
FLAILING	BARBARIAN	DEPRECATION	REVOLUTIONARY	CAVERNOUS
REVULSION	ENVIOUS	FREE SPACE	ASSURANCE	MEAGER
PROSTRATE	GHASTLY	DISTRACTEDLY	EXULTANT	ACCOMPLICE
PARSON	PETULANCE	PERILOUS	GALLING	SUBMISSION

Tuck Everlasting Vocabulary

METAPHYSICS	LUXURIOUS	INFINITE	OPPRESSIVE	TEEMING
SEDATELY	EXTRAORDINARY	INDOMITABLE	RUEFUL	TRANQUIL
ACRID	GANDER	FREE SPACE	SKELTER	MARIONETTE
CONSOLINGLY	ACCOMMODATIONS	IMMENSE	TANGENT	ORDEAL
FORLORN	MELANCHOLY	DECISIVELY	IRRELEVANTLY	PERIL

www.ingramcontent.com/pod-product-compliance
Lightning Source LLC
Chambersburg PA
CBHW081455070526
44586CB00019B/2367